Write, Think,

Find out how to create the climate and space for everyday student writing. In this new co-publication with MiddleWeb, award-winning teacher Mary Tedrow shows you how to encourage students to integrate daily writing into their lives, leading to improved critical thinking skills, increased knowledge of subject areas, and greater confidence in written expression. This practical guide will help you consider the unique needs of your students, while still meeting state standards.

You'll discover how to . . .

♦ Develop classroom routines and activities that invite creativity and self-expression
♦ Teach writing methods that can be used across different grade levels and all content areas
♦ Challenge students to examine their own writing processes for thinking and problem solving
♦ Evaluate written work in a way that emphasizes growth over grades

Many exercises, prompts, and attempts at thinking found in the book can be easily adapted for use both in and out of the classroom. Whether you are a new or experienced teacher, *Write, Think, Learn* will enable you to make writing come alive for all your students.

Mary K. Tedrow is a National Board Certified Teacher of English Language Arts/Adolescence and Young Adulthood with twenty-six years of classroom experience. She directs the Shenandoah Valley Writing Project housed at Shenandoah University.

Write, Think, Learn

Tapping the Power of Daily Student Writing Across the Content Areas

Mary K. Tedrow

Routledge
Taylor & Francis Group

NEW YORK AND LONDON

MiddleWeb
All About the Middle Grades

First published 2018
by Routledge
711 Third Avenue, New York, NY 10017

and by Routledge
2 Park Square, Milton Park, Abingdon, Oxon, OX14 4RN

Routledge is an imprint of the Taylor & Francis Group, an informa business

Library of Congress Cataloging-in-Publication Data
A catalog record for this book has been requested

ISBN: 978-1-138-05270-3 (hbk)
ISBN: 978-1-138-05277-2 (pbk)
ISBN: 978-1-315-16757-2 (ebk)

Typeset in Palatino
by Apex CoVantage, LLC

Visit the eResources: www.routledge.com/9781138052772

Contents

eResources

The tools and handouts in Appendix B and Appendix C will also be available as free eResources 🔽, so you can easily download and print them for classroom use.

You can access them by visiting the book product page: www.routledge. com/9781138052772. Click on the tab that says "eResources" and select the files. They will begin downloading to your computer.

Meet the Author

Mary K. Tedrow is a National Board Certified Teacher of English Language Arts/Adolescence and Young Adulthood with twenty-six years of classroom experience. She is also Director of the Shenandoah Valley Writing Project, served as a commissioner on the National Education Association Commission on Effective Teachers and Teaching, and is a charter member of the Center for Teaching Quality Teacher Leaders Forum (now the CTQ Collaboratory).

Mary has written for *Teacher* Magazine, Aspen Publishers, the National Writing Project *Quarterly*, and other outlets. Her past experience includes advertising copywriting for companies such as Rubbermaid and American Woodmark. She maintains a blog at www.walkingtoschool.blogspot.com. Her teaching has been recognized for excellence as a District Teacher of the Year; the awarding of the first Porterfield Endowed English Chair at John Handley High School in Winchester, Virginia; as well as Inspiring Educator 2012 and the Distinguished Alumni Award for Professional Achievement in 2013 by Shenandoah University.

Acknowledgments

This book would not be possible without the generous sharing of colleagues, friends, mentors, and students. The model of the National Writing Project followed closely by my home site, the Northern Virginia Writing Project, nurtures a verdant community where educators share a combined knowledge of classroom practice. In the hands and minds of the dedicated teachers of the Summer Institutes, the world of the classroom is revealed as endlessly fascinating, energizing, curious, and dynamic.

Thank you to my first department chair, Meta Potts, who brought the Northern Virginia Writing Project to our school in 1981. It is here, after my K–12 and university schooling was over, that I learned what writing really is all about.

Theresa Manchey is the mentor and friend who pushed me to enter the Invitational Summer Institute where I began to harvest good instruction from the teachers of the network. The climate of sharing she fostered as an English department chair at James Wood High School still stands as a model for success.

Thank you to fellow teacher consultants Kim Sloan, Susan McGilvray, Laura Tucker, Mary Bowser, and countless others who have shared their best lessons and their thoughtful guidance as we puzzle our way through teaching, trying our best to assist students in finding a voice and a purpose.

To my summer writing groups, thank you, thank you. Chapter 2 was honed under the watchful eye of career teachers Heidi Branch of Belmont Ridge Middle School, Christopher Brown of Battlefield High School, and Sarah Grace MulQueen of Longfellow Middle School.

Chapter 1 was a part of every writing group meeting with Nicole Korsen of Dominion High School, Lisa Larkin of P. B. Smith Elementary, and Jacqueline Mutz of Rock Ridge High School.

Get yourself into a writing group with other teachers. They are brilliant.

Many thanks go to my amazing students from James Wood High School, Dowell J. Howard Technical School, Millbrook High School, and John Handley High School where students were always willing to take risks with me. I am especially grateful to the former students who lent me their words and images for inclusion in this text. I am always grateful to have known all of you. Students have enriched my life beyond expression.

Thanks also goes to my family. My husband, Lynn, read drafts, listened to my ruminations, and fed me. Thanks also to our three children—Annie, Neil, and Carolyn—who taught me to love kid watching at any age and have now provided me with many grandchildren so I can continue my studies.

Finally, I would like to thank John Norton. He has been a continual support and encouragement since we met digitally in 2001. John has shepherded many teachers into the role of author. He is truly a teacher of teachers, though he claims the title of editor. He has shown his faith in teacher knowledge through his MiddleWeb site and through the numbers of teacher-authors he has encouraged to write their own texts. John truly believes that teachers have a fund of untapped knowledge. I am grateful beyond words for his support and friendship over the years.

Preface

How to Read This Book

Teachers juggle multiple, sometimes conflicting, demands: meet the needs of a diverse group of students through differentiation, but get everyone to the finish line in time for a scheduled, standardized test. Devote time to assess and reassess student learning and plan to fill in gaps in skill or understanding while getting everyone to that looming deadline. We turn ourselves inside out assessing, reviewing, and collecting data. But an easy resolution is right in front of us that lets us assess on the go and make adjustments in the moment. *Writing* is a tool which both differentiates and engages every student in their comfort zone. It deepens and personalizes learning for every student. It is also a window into the mind, revealing where misconceptions, misunderstandings, and even grand applications of knowledge are immediately accessible. Our students' writings tell us where we need to go next. This is data that reaches far beyond a data point.

Writing helps us learn in any content. When we write, we transform thoughts into symbolic representation on paper. The very act of writing forces us to process and engage. But writing tasks are often left for the English teacher. There are complaints that writing takes too long and is difficult to grade. When writing is used in the content, many rely on it solely as an assessment tool—a summative essay or report. Most teachers encountered writing this way in their own schooling: as a tool for testing. Grading these products is indeed labor intensive on the teacher's part, particularly if student writing is rife with lapses in thought and control.

But writing can be used for a variety of purposes: for recording, reflecting, processing experience, and collecting and formulating ideas. And many of these opportunities to write require little scoring effort on the part of the teacher. Regular informal, quickly composed, and immediately shared writings build the intellectual behaviors we want to see in our students. Daily practice in writing for learning reveals a hidden curriculum—those habits of mind and motive that some students learn through osmosis. Others flounder through school, lacking the tools that help them learn. We can reveal these hidden processes through frequent, informal writings that run parallel to thought processes, replacing standard note taking and fill-in-the blank with authentic learning. The added benefit is that a daily writing habit, just like a daily reading habit, improves student literacy skills in every content.

When *replacing* lecture with writing in the content, we also invite student voice into the examination of information. Frequent practice, followed by regular sharing of written thoughts, will flush out the knowledge students bring with them. Experts appear from thin air. Students see each other as sources or as demonstrators of attainable skills in that special "zone of proximal development" that Lev Vygotsky identified as the magic, secret sauce of social learning. When we write and share, we open our classrooms to embrace a community of learners, all helping one another head in the same direction.

But "constructed responses"—or written answers to questions—can be difficult to manage if you are a secondary teacher who works with 100 or more students. How can you possibly handle the paper load?

This book is about bringing together the promise of student writing with the realities of serving many students in every discipline. It is for the English teacher as well as the history, science, music, athletic, or related arts teacher. Writing helps us learn in any content. Forming the habit of reflection in writing and goal setting is a lifelong skill you can make available to both your students and yourself.

If you have begun reading this book, then you have already taken the most important first step: joining with other teachers to grow and shape your understanding about writing as a tool. Teaching, like learning, is best done in collaboration with others, and this text is a compilation of many voices from a long career of listening to and learning from those who strive to help students enjoy the promise of education—a chance to know and understand ourselves and the world we live in. The most exhilarating discussions and readings of my career have been in the company of caring and energized teachers. Let this book be a further entry to the ongoing conversations around supporting students in our quest that they gain a sense of themselves as a maker of meaning—a writer.

Do not think of this book as the *only* method for encouraging writing every day with your students, but as a manageable starting point for embracing a new way of looking at writing to discover that all students can produce meaningful written work, given the appropriate space and time. Each teacher will want to adapt strategies to fit their specific teaching environment. However, sometimes just getting started is the biggest obstacle.

As with any new process, including writing, I encourage you to simply begin. There is ample time for revision of instruction in the months and years after beginning. Simply starting daily writing with students will force a search for opportunities to prompt student thinking. One success with student thinking will lead to more. Feel free to mimic every step or to discard half and make the rest your own. Careful observation of your students will tell you what you need to do next.

Here Is How to Get the Most From This Book

If you are already sold on the idea of writing in your content, but are unsure of how to employ this tool in your classroom, then skip Chapter 1 and move right on to Chapter 2. Chapter 2 provides explicit directions for launching students into the habit of writing every day. It provides student motivation as well as tips to manage the classroom environment.

If you are not yet convinced that providing time in the classroom for daily writing is worth the time, read Chapter 1. This chapter provides examples of how writing influences student self-efficacy and understanding of content, while inviting students into the community of learners we hope they will forge together. It follows my journey to create a vibrant, caring, growing community of learners and explores the underlying theory for regular, exploratory writing.

Teachers in every content will find material worth reviewing in Chapters 3, 4, 5, and 6.

- ◆ Chapter 3 helps instructors understand effective prompting. The most effective prompts are nearly invisible. These inspire students to write without even thinking of the task as a "writing assignment." Prompts are also broken down into four discernible purposes. When asking students to write, it is very helpful to know what you hope to accomplish through the writing. This purpose-driven knowledge shapes the prompt as well as any assessment of how well students are doing in reaching curricular goals. Each of the following chapters (4, 5, 6, and 7) focuses on one of the stated purposes for prompting. Each reflects an intellectual behavior we want our students to practice.
- ◆ Chapter 4 helps teachers employ daily writing for *setting goals and reflecting* on learning.
- ◆ Chapter 5 offers prompts to help students *think critically*. The main purpose for these prompts is to build student confidence in their own observations and the ability to generate original thoughts rather than letting the "experts" do all the thinking.
- ◆ Chapter 6 focuses on prompts to *help students understand and absorb concepts in the content area*. English language arts teachers will find many prompts that help students engage with reading and

writing concepts, since I spent my career locating, stealing, and developing these tools for my classroom. However, most of these are adapted for other content areas. Use these reliable techniques while indulging in a kleptomaniac search for prompts that do the double duty of both teaching and forming written thought.

◆ Chapter 7 will be useful for teachers who ask students to create *major summative papers* in the course and are looking for ways to get students into and through the process. These prompts help students collect thinking over time. The traditional use of a writer's notebook is as a tool for collected thought. All content teachers should help students generate ideas long before final papers are due. Many opportunities to write also provide an opportunity for students to choose from among their best ideas. Teaching a process for collecting and developing papers, for revising and incorporating resources, is necessary in any content when a written product is required.

The final chapter in the book, Chapter 8, deals primarily with a teacher's central question: Do I have to read and grade all of this? Hopefully, by the time a teacher reaches Chapter 8 about *assessment*, it is obvious that assessing the writing has been continual and ongoing, especially if teachers are putting student writing immediately to work in the classroom.

This book is a compilation of *what I think I know now* about daily writing and how it can create a kinder, more inclusive learning environment. The ideas are a compilation of my teaching, informed by the practices and ideas of many of my peers who you will meet throughout the pages. These conversations and techniques have the power to transform the learning environment because they are rooted in composition theory resulting from a studied practice of real writers and thinkers, but which have proven to work well with our novice, student writers.

Through writing and sharing we come to know our students, and they come to know us as caring, respectful, trustworthy, and optimistic authorities. When we hear student thinking, we begin to trust them to take on the responsibility for learning, often reaching far beyond our immediate curricular goals.

1

Why Add Writing?

Moving to Community and Authentic Learning

"Tell me, and I forget. Teach me, and I remember. Involve me, and I learn."
—Benjamin Franklin

What to Expect

This chapter focuses on what daily writing looks like in a classroom, explaining why teachers might want to incorporate this practice into a course that already has many curricular demands. Even the hardest to reach students find success when certain parameters are in place. Besides students, teachers also suffer from a wariness of writing from their own history, tending to avoid the task in the classroom. A rationale for moving past our history is included.

Chapter Topics

- ◆ Exemplifying authentic writing and its power to transform students.
- ◆ Ensuring student success with choice, time, and a valued audience.
- ◆ Understanding why students and adults struggle with a self-image of "writer."
- ◆ Employing the Daybook to enhance writing skills and learning.

Success With Real Writing Versus Assigned Writing

Through the annual challenges of creating a high school master schedule, my journalism course was whittled down to one student: a faithful returning editor. The co-editor, unable to fit the class in her schedule, signed on to work during my planning period. Though there were only two students, we all wanted the paper to continue.

What to do? My colleague across the hall and I concocted a plan. She was facing a huge co-taught class, overrun with hyperactive boys. We would divide and conquer. Any student who volunteered could work with me in the lab twice a week to create the school newspaper.

After presenting the prospect of writing for the newspaper to the entire class, "the boys," a notorious, but much loved group of brawling, loud, exuberant, cursing, attention-deficit, special education, senior boys who had known each another most of their school lives, enthusiastically volunteered to take on the job. They would comprise the staff, and on a reduced schedule, we would continue to publish to the entire school.

The year was an endless parade of outside-the-box events. One boy quietly mummified himself with masking tape while a team planning discussion diverted our attention. We had to enact a fine for cursing overload, even though the boys would willingly contribute to the kitty when they felt they could express themselves no other way.

One of our reporters showed up, not once but twice, with scarred knuckles, and finally a broken hand, from punching concrete walls when his girlfriend upset him. Another exhausted the digital camera battery by mindlessly clicking the fire button so frequently in a walk from the room to the parking lot that he had to return for a charged battery before even beginning the assignment.

But the paper came out on schedule and featured their articles, photographs, advertisements, and commentary. They interviewed, wrote, revised, edited, devised cut lines, learned the publishing software, and then celebrated when they delivered their issues school wide.

Though the boys surprised me in many ways, they never stopped teaching me what happens when students are trusted to follow their interests and are given the time and latitude to see a vision through to completion. They will work hard. *Really hard*.

For instance, a student transfer from another state with a severe language disability showed up in the lab at the end of school one day. "What are you doing here?" I asked. "Weren't you out sick today?"

"I have an interview scheduled, and I need the camera." Ka-ching! went my teacher brain, though I just smiled and handed him the camera.

He took meticulous notes. Later, while composing his story, I spent about five minutes showing him how to correctly punctuate quotes. He then stayed rooted to the chair for two hours, carefully fixing every quote. His mother, who worked in the cafeteria, described his rising pride and self-confidence to me on more than one occasion, especially after his byline appeared in print.

Henry, a self-declared fan of hallway fights, became our food columnist. In addition to fights, he was also a huge fan of food, critiquing everything from the school lunch menu to the local Waffle House. After his effusive praise for Waffle House ran, it was picked up and reprinted in the chain's national newsletter.

The other boys found their interests as well. Joseph, the wrestler, took over the sports page, sharing the duties with two other boys. In addition to covering the traditional school sports, they added features on non-school-related sports. They diligently caught up with and followed a group who spent afternoons playing disk golf. Conducting the interviews and taking pictures was done on their own time.

After senior year, they went their separate ways, a couple to a college where their Individual Education Plan needs were supported and others into construction or other trades. Meanwhile, the newspaper went off for judging.

In October, after the results of the evaluation arrived, we tracked the boys down for a reunion so they could accept praise from the school board for the first-place ranking awarded by state evaluators. Their undisciplined entrance to the staid meeting was no less characteristic than all the other entrances they had made to every classroom throughout their school careers.

I could not have been prouder. Not only had the boys earned the first-place ranking, they had shown that, given the right conditions and support, all students can view themselves as writers.

The Challenge in the Classroom

This whole eventful year only highlighted a continual struggle to equate successes in the journalism lab with those in my regular English classroom. In regular English, we slogged through assigned writings. The process felt fake—everyone going through the motions of producing print read by one person: me. The atmosphere was wooden, unlike the vibrant, chatty newsroom. I wanted all my classrooms to feel like the journalism lab where there was laughter, sharing, some very frustrating struggles—and lots of learning. Routinely there was far more growth realized in the journalism class than in the "regular" classroom. The boys were just further proof that something had to give in the traditional language arts classes.

Somehow, I needed to harness the interest, autonomy, pride, joy, and ultimate language arts growth—not to mention self-efficacy growth—that was fostered in creating a newspaper to be read by the entire student body.

The qualities that seemed to help the boys succeed were the same ones heralded by the two Dons—Graves and Murray, early instructors and illuminators of process writing:

- ◆ Choice—Students made their own assignments.
- ◆ An authentic audience—Students were writing for a valued audience: their peers.
- ◆ Time—Though we turned out an issue a month and time was squeezed, the bulk of class time was given over to production, not lecture. They had time to get their projects done. I also had time to sit beside individuals and ask questions to shape both their assignments and their writing. The lab reveals writing as a social and problem-solving act where all the students and the instructor are involved in the final product. Additionally, during *really* engaging work, students create their own time: coming in after school, working on weekends. They also had time throughout the year to practice the skills repeatedly, rather the one and done mindset of the classroom. They were getting lots of supported coaching.

And yet, back in the regular classroom, there was the curriculum. We have things students should learn about the development of good literature. I could not have a newspaper running in every class. There wouldn't be enough time to meet my other obligations. Still, I kept looking for ways to incorporate the student energy and gains I saw every day in the lab. This *could* be fun, engaging, and self-directed. All students could muster the energy to surmount problems in composition if they cared enough. We *could* see real growth, if only I could figure out how.

I knew all my students needed these experiences or they might never come to view themselves as competent *writers*—people who put pen to paper or fingers to keyboard because they have something to say—even if it's just about the last meal they ate. Time and again, students like the boys, who had been written off as incapable, had proven otherwise after discovering a written voice and a valuable audience. The key would be to help students find that voice and audience. Without that, they would end up like the adults in my night class.

Teaching Wounded Writers

In addition to the courses at the high school, I led a graduate course called "Writing to Learn." Course participants study composition theory while working on their own writing. Routinely, before publicly sharing a first writing, the adult learners reach out privately. They almost form a line before that first night, either digitally or in person. Confessions abound. "I'm not really very good at writing," I hear again and again. Few adults, it appears, escape school without thinking of themselves as very poor writers. They all ask for understanding, leniency. "I'm not very good at writing," they say. I hear: "Be nice to me. I have a gaping, painful wound from my own writing education."

For the most part, these adults—all teachers who are exploring the use of writing as a tool for learning with their students—have had the same kind of writing education I did, a faulty one.

A History of Avoidance Tactics

Here's an analogy: Imagine being handed a basketball, placed on a team, and thrust on a court to play in a high-stakes, championship game. There has been no practice or warm-up—just a few directions like "Run toward the basket while bouncing the ball simultaneously, weave around people, and put it in the net." While playing the game, rabid fans will be booing every mistake—and, clearly, there will be many. Very quickly most would conclude they are very bad basketball players. In fact, most would do as much as possible to avoid ever playing in a game like that again.

Like basketball, writing is a skill that requires hours of practice, coaching, and feedback for successful improvement. But like the basketball game, we often put our students in the same situation as our hypothetical player. We give them directions (a formula), a topic they did not choose (the assignment), and a tournament-style writing situation (a grade for a course or a standardized test). Neither situation makes us feel that we are either good basketball players or good writers. Like the adults in the night class, there will be lots of writing avoidance and a poor self-image.

Of course, some of our students are naturals, like gifted athletes, but most are going to need some help. But even gifted athletes will have their natural abilities honed through many hours of practice. It's true that we will not all become professional basketball players or best-selling authors, but we should be able to play a passing game with some sense of confidence. After all, sports are good for our health, and writing is good for employment, reflection, gathering ideas, sorting through experiences, and even dealing with trauma. Additionally, the basics of good written expression are more and more a necessity for negotiating an increasingly complex world as we send and receive messages throughout the day. If you don't play basketball, you should at least know a good game when you see one and should recognize a good piece of writing when you read it. And you may not write the great American novel, but you could appreciate the craft of producing one after working through your own writing process. In any case, practice rather than avoidance will always move participants closer to mastery.

A Skill Demanding Practice

Too often both students and adults have a distaste for writing primarily because they have not done enough of it. And what they've done has been scrutinized long before it was ready for inspection. In school, much of writing is still assigned, and then graded, with an eye to finding deficiency—lots of booing. In addition, little time and support—or coaching, to follow the sports analogy—is offered. After many mistakes, students equate writing with spelling and grammar rather than finding a voice for self-expression. No wonder we all lack confidence.

Currently, high-stakes testing of written products throughout the school years have prompted many teachers—who often feel uncomfortable as writers themselves (these are my adult learners who self-describe as poor writers) to return to formulaic essay preparation, scoring against a prescribed and constrictive rubric and abandoning the more open-ended, process writing to push everyone over a low bar.

Complaints do not end at the English classroom door. In other content areas colleagues complain of written student products. "They can't write!" I'm told. What I'm thinking is that the student likely doesn't know what they are writing about nor have they been provided time to shape a nascent idea into a fully fledged thesis. Like the basketball game, we can't just talk to students about playing and then hand them a ball and expect them to join the winning team at tournament time. Students need a place to explore and rehearse their thinking in all the content areas too, figuring out large concepts long before they are asked to form an argument, devise a solution, or apply new thinking.

Back in the Real World

Tangled prose is an indication of tangled thinking. It isn't the writing that suffers. It is the thought. This has been clear for a long time: Hugh Blair wrote the following in in 1801:

> We may rest assured that, whenever we express ourselves ill, there is, besides the mismanagement of language, for the most part some mistake in our manner of conceiving the subject. Embarrassed, obscure, and feeble sentences are generally, if not always, the result of embarrassed, obscure, and feeble thought. . . . He that is learning to arrange his sentences with accuracy and order is learning, at the same time, to think with accuracy and order.
>
> (p. 154)

Even poor writing by students provides an insight: they aren't getting it.

The goal for my regular English classrooms was to carve out of our already crowded curriculum a safe space for the practice runs and drills needed to build the muscles for both writing and thinking. My tool for achieving this became the Daybook, a standard feature of nearly every class meeting and the vehicle leading students to consider themselves writers, sometimes for the first time in their schooling career. The activities have stimulated students in all the English classes from the co-taught ELL and SPED classes to the Advanced Placement literature and language courses. For the over 50% free and reduced lunch students at our school—those generally identified as low socio-economic status—the Daybook can become the place to process the lives they are negotiating between home and school. For them, learning to write in a safe space can literally be a life preserver—a way to deal with multiple stressors in their lives. In addition, the student writing leads them into a deeper understanding of literary devices and writer's craft and is a safe space for teasing out areas of expertise or interest for assigned projects.

Prompting in the Daybook features an opportunity for every child to write about something personally meaningful connected to content. This is one of the features of a well-rounded literacy program that every child should be exposed to every day (Allington and Gabirel, p. 11). Daily writing also prompts daily thinking.

Our Daybook in Context

"Okay. Get out your Daybooks and turn to the next blank page. Date your entry. Today is November 2."

A muffled cheer rises from the class. "I love these things," Ashley says in the void. Though she has leaned into her friend nearby, I can hear. We *all* can hear. But the consensus seems to be that we all agree. Daybook entries are fun. That's partly the point. A sense of play infuses our daily practice before we take ourselves seriously enough to devote time and energy to the daunting task of getting writing right.

Our class has been too busy the past few days to tackle the Daybook, so their enthusiasm at this familiar routine is warming. For Ashley, this commentary is huge. She tenuously entered Advanced Placement stating she was "not very good at writing" and had previously avoided the challenge of upper academic work. Both she and her mother expressed concern over demands of the course. "She struggles with writing. She is worried about keeping up, but she insisted on taking the challenge," her mother confides at the school Open House. Under her confession I hear the mother's plea: "Please don't be too hard on her. She's trying. She's scared."

For Ashley, as we made writing a central feature of our daily meetings, her confidence grew, primarily because she discovered her own voice and the realization that she truly has something to say in a risk-free zone, her Daybook. Ashley has also been part of a supportive writing group of friends. She has heard and read their writing on an almost daily basis. The mystery and possibility of writing has been revealed. No longer has Ashley compared herself only to the professional mentor texts that she has read over the years that reveal none of the messiness of producing great literature. Her mentors are peers, and what they have done she thinks she can handle.

In addition, she has been encouraged throughout the course to bring in her outside interests. In her case, this has included a love of horses. Ashley's passion has inspired attempts at both poetry and essay to reveal what working with impressive animals has meant to her. Horses she knows. She *can* write about that. And if she can write about that, she can write. Her image of herself as a writer has grown. Having found and built confidence in this knowledge, she chose the poem "After a Rainstorm" by Robert Wrigley for the course's challenging poetry explication paper: "Because I have come to the fence at night, / The horses arrive also from their ancient stable" (Wrigley, l. 1–2). The lines of the poem draw her in through a familiar experience. The resulting explication was a mature, academic paper replete with a knowing voice where her experiences were married to the voice of the poem. She had bridged the gap from the personal to the academic and was justly proud of the outcome.

The Daybook for students operates the same way it operates for real writers. The term "Daybook" is taken from esteemed writing instructor Donald Murray, and for him it was the genesis for most of his writing, which included a Pulitzer Prize for commentary. It is a tool for locating and capturing fleeting thoughts, for experimenting with ideas before taking them forward, as a safe space for trying various techniques and topics in writing without the fear of evaluation, while also serving as a valuable tool for processing and reflecting on experience. As Murray argued, any writing will lead to the discovery of new thinking. The writing itself engenders thought.

In the classroom, students rehearse academic papers, discover words to describe themselves for Personal Statements, engage in thinking around issues affecting their lives, and continually dump the contents of their brains onto a stark white page to literally see what they have to say.

When we start the year, initial entries help students locate their own reasons for regular writing—shifting the responsibility for practice from the instructor to the student. As we progress, classroom prompts are a deliberate method to help students find topics or rehearse conclusions. The journal is the place to collect these tender beginnings; it is the kindling for a much larger fire later. By collecting revision ideas and new discoveries, the writing surprises as it frees students from too-early judgment.

As I embraced the need for daily writing as a way to improve the more purposeful assigned writing, prompting became more directed toward connecting writing to the lesson for the day and linking their writing to our discussions. For instance, our writing before discussion helps students actively locate their own thoughts before being influenced by more extroverted talkers. Discussions are richer and more organic. I began prompting with questions I wanted them to use for thinking in writing before sharing. Then we shared, first with a partner and then on to a large group discussion. Everyone gets the opportunity to flesh out thoughts. Because we write routinely, the students see the regular activity less as writing, with a capital W, and more as the vehicle for recording thought.

Returning Creativity and Thinking to Students

Another offshoot of regular writing and sharing is a return to a sense of joy, where students are allowed the same freedom to create and experiment they had when they arrived in kindergarten. Students delight in hearing their peers. One bold and highly successful reading of student text leads others to experiment. When a student reader receives positive feedback, through laughter, applause, or nods, this tacit approval builds confidence. In all English classes students need confidence in their observations and opinions if they are to build solid arguments and analyses that emerge from their thinking rather than relying on cutting and pasting from other vaunted sources.

Additionally, the best writing activities help students find "a way in" to a lesson or topic. Daniel Willingham, author of *Why Don't Students Like School?* (2009) says that this type of activity, one which is new and just slightly beyond reach but that ultimately ends in a student-generated solution, makes learning fun and encourages learners to return for more. When topics are too far out of student reach, many students only experience frustration rather than the satisfaction of succeeding in a task. Daily writing prompts that let students join their experience to the task result in that satisfaction, and the entire activity becomes pleasurable.

Ultimately, I hope the students absorb one truth: writing is more than establishing a thesis with three limited supporting ideas backed up with examples. Writing is an expression of thinking: *original and creative thinking*. Writers feel moved to record because they have something to *say*. Helping students find what it is they want to say is yet another goal of the daily writing. We practice speaking in our own individual voices and discovering and naming our own individual ideas. It is a hotbed of personal thinking and a place for daily drills in moving our metaphorical basketball down the court.

Goals for the Daily Writing

The Daybook, a tool I continue to refine, is presented here in its current form but is always under revision, particularly as I experiment with new prompts as entry points. The prompts that result in greater understanding are retained, while other experimental, less successful prompts are discarded. There is continual experimentation on my part and any teacher who hopes to embed this in their course can expect to need a method of tracking what works for students and what should be abandoned. (Your own Daybook is the likely tool for this.) I also retain the right to continually revise my teaching, just as we do our writing.

Writers at any level, adults or children, benefit from a classroom geared toward these objectives:

- ◆ Kids need to write far more than we can grade to improve. Daily writing produces pages and pages of student text.
- ◆ Kids need to discover their own thinking because writing is not about correctness exclusively, but about having something to say. They need space to figure out what they have to say.
- ◆ Kids need to discover their written voice. Students are encouraged to just "read what you wrote" so they can hear how they sound on paper.
- ◆ We all need somewhere to try and fail—to take risks without being evaluated on those risks. Much of schooling does not offer rehearsal space. The Daybook is a psychological safe zone for experimenting with challenging topics or a foreign genre.
- ◆ Kids need to enter new ideas through their own experience and begin the thinking primarily in their home language, that which is closest to speech. The Daybook is where we collect all that thinking around curriculum.
- ◆ Writer's notebooks in many forms help students live as writers. This enhances their understanding of reading. We try many of the techniques we see the writers using, and we practice to improve student-generated text. Ultimately, this writing helps students become better readers, noticing what writers do. Journals in a specific discipline foster the same inside-out understanding of writing in history, science, math, or any of the creative arts.
- ◆ Kids need to write in a pressure-free zone to produce creatively and with some level of confidence.

During Ashley's remark about her love of the Daybook prompts, and others like it throughout the day, I indulge in an inward smile. This is the kind of feedback *I* live for—students enjoying an activity in class—any activity, really, where they express both delight and wonder and sometimes surprise. My colleagues and I coined a term for this: *sneaky-hard.* It is a classroom activity kids jump on without realizing that they are about to dive into an intellectual problem. Ultimately, they work harder, that is more deeply, than they have on the "hard" stuff (memorizing long lists of terms, reading hundreds of assigned pages). In survey after survey, and in comments to other students and teachers, my students say, "Your class is fun, but it makes me think." I'll take that one. Learning *should* be both fun and thoughtful. If it is pleasurable, we might want to do it again rather than invent avoidance tactics that keep us off the basketball court.

Back in the Real World

What students say about their Daybooks:

"It was a struggle at first, to begin writing 'free' pieces. Then I realized that I have so many thoughts that I have never written down. Writing became so much more fun. . . . I am so incredibly glad that I was given this chance because I now love writing stories!" —George, senior

"I was shocked to find that I had written approximately fifty pages worth of material for this class. Never in my life did I think I could approach that page limit in years, but I have proven myself wrong by doing it in a mere semester." —Sam, senior

"My personal writings show what I can do when I am given the freedom to write about whatever I want. The reader should be able to notice a greater emotional attachment to these writings. For many of these I poured my heart out onto the paper, and I think I may have been able to transfer some of those feelings onto the paper. My writings are the culmination of my true person, what I really think about certain things, and how I truly act. The personal writings are some of the most creative writing that I have ever done." —David, senior

"The daybook has been a great tool to use in developing my writing ability. Prior to this I had almost no experience with journaling. I was able to try a wide variety of writing styles, especially with poetry." —Anna, senior

"This semester I have been fairly religious about keeping up my daybook. I have filled 190 of 200 pages in my composition notebook with my large, messy handwriting and plan to fill the last ten before the year is over. In fact, I found that I enjoyed keeping a daybook so much that I have already purchased a new one, and intend to try to keep this up as a daily practice." ——Cassie, senior

"This section contains personal writings that are still rough. They're ideas, just not in the format that I want them to be in. A few are excerpts from my daybook, and there is also a poem, probably one of the very first ones I've written that was a prompt. I enjoy these types of pieces though. Similar to unprompted writing assignments, I grew to love writing through these pieces, but in a different way. These types of writings are for me to discuss my thoughts with myself. It is for me to learn from myself and by myself. A type of enlightenment that comes from solitude." —Carter, senior

Return Learning to Students

Too often in school we take ownership of all the thinking, planning, and construction of student work. The Daybook has been the tool mined, honed, and adjusted over the years to return this work to our students. Real writers write because they have something to *say*. The Daybook helps students find their own voice.

Two years after the boys in the journalism lab graduated, I was surprised to encounter Joseph, the wrestler, coming up the basement stairs at a home where I was a guest for a meeting. "Oh, of course, Louise is Joseph's mother," I thought. I hadn't really put it together. After a big hug and some catching up on what Joseph had been doing away at school, he left with some of his friends.

"I didn't think you were ever one of his teachers," Louise confessed.

"Well, technically, I wasn't. My name would never have been on the report card." I went on to tell her how we had pulled the boys out twice a week to work on the paper.

"Oh! You did the paper? Let me tell you about that. Every time one of the papers was published, all the boys would gather here at the house. They read the articles out loud to each other and then they always said together and to each other, 'See, we're not dumb.'"

Oh, my.

If we don't get kids writing and thinking for any other reason, let it be because we can't keep letting kids leave school thinking they are dumb.

Summing Up

If we want students to view themselves as writers, or "makers of meaning," we need to provide the time and tools for both invention and practice. Writing is an exercise in constructing understanding and should be practiced within the confines of each discipline. Students need a chance to both think and write in connection to new material. The Daybook is a tool for giving every student, no matter the skill level, the time, space, and comfort, to get in touch with their thinking in your course. In addition, the much-needed practice will result in better writing skill, a personalized sense of the content, and a more complete idea of what it means to compose with words.

For the Daybook, Incorporate the Following:

- ◆ Provide choice, time, and a valued audience so students will expend the energy needed to develop a written product.
- ◆ Offer time for practice. Writing is a skill. Most students do not get enough writing practice to improve on their writing fluency. We are fluent writers when we easily produce written thought without fear or anxiety.
- ◆ Configure daily writing to include the goals of the curriculum. Think of daily writing as an "instead of" and not an "add on."
- ◆ Keep the Daybook flexible enough to capture all kinds of written thought.

The next chapter explains how to get started in your classroom with this valuable practice.

2

Where to Begin?

Motivating Students to Accept the Daily Writing Challenge

"Motivation is the art of getting people to do what you want them to do because they want to do it."

—Dwight D. Eisenhower

What to Expect

This chapter is about setting up the routines and supports for daily writing in a classroom. Within are the lessons I have used with great success to excite students about daily writing—even writing that goes beyond the school day. The lessons help students embrace writing as a tool to improve their learning, their lives, their creativity, and, ultimately, their skill as a writer. I want students excited as well as challenged to adopt a new practice from the very beginning of our time together. The first few days of introducing the Daybook provide a flexible framework that develops, manages, facilitates, assesses, and reflects on student thought.

Chapter Topics

◆ Introducing, formatting, and managing the notebook.
◆ Motivating students to set a purpose for the daily writing *and* a course of study.
◆ Developing routines that support success in a classroom that writes.

Slow Down Initially, Speed Up Later

Students grow to value their Daybooks when *we* value them by both conferring the gift of time and honoring them as personal spaces. Additionally, frequent use of the Daybook in the classroom routine emphasizes its importance as a place to discover a written voice, to maintain a record of our changing thinking, as a private space to make sense of the world, and as a location for grappling with concepts of content before going public on a graded essay or test. To truly cement daily writing as a habit, teachers can assist students in initiating and maintaining the habit by tying an inherent value to the activity. Starting the year with these goals in mind is the purpose of the introductory lessons. Spend time on the lessons so reliable routines are in place to free students to think around concepts. Routines provide a steady framework to support student risk taking in writing.

But how do you start something new? Change a habit? Create buy in? Over the years it has been clear that the introduction to the Daybook cannot be shortchanged. Convincing students that they will like and value this writing space is the ultimate objective, and I am not above using marketing tools to my advantage. Just like building an argument in prose, draw on ethos, pathos, and logos to box students in to the realization that daily writing can be fun, energizing, of personal value, and a surefire way to "meet yourself" and your personal, unique perspective. The opening lessons cannot be overstated—they will either convince a student to take on the challenge or fall flat.

Having said all that, not every student completes the challenge of writing daily. Some struggle with forming this new habit. Others may not value the process until much later, even though they complied at the time. But even if the daily writing challenge is not fully met, these are students who will write more during this class than any they have in the past. We must take that as a win too.

Back in the Real World

Before the school day begins, I rush to the main office to collect copies. On the way, I pass through the senior cafeteria. In one corner is Kyle from the fall semester, no longer enrolled in English 12. He is writing in his Daybook. I have seen him here many times before. The cover is a distinctive black leather—one he selected for himself—and, because he's shared some passages with me in the past, I know it includes drawings, reflections, and plans all in a neat, tightly spaced, block print. He wants to be an engineer. Some of the drawings are schematics. All are accompanied by his thoughts.

He sits off to the side in a quiet corner, but he is here nearly every day, writing. This is clearly part of his daily routine. Writing in the Daybook is a new habit we formed together as part of our meetings in the first semester. Though a confident writer when he entered the course, Kyle was a serious-minded student who saw little use for the creative process. By allowing him to set his own personal goals for the daily writing, he quickly saw value in holding on to a written record of the ideas that passed fleetingly through his mind during the day, as is evidenced by his continued use of the Daybook. His notebook includes drawings and commentary, all of which enhance his career aspiration.

I exhibit excitement while presenting each of my arguments, drawing on personal experience, research, songwriters, artists, anyone I can find who has testified to their own composing process. Daily writing does not need to be a chore, or the vegetables you must eat before dessert. It is the main course: a free, open space to explore and create an understanding of content and the world. It is a delicious opportunity to think loudly on paper, to make sense of experience, to dream, to explore. My job—your job, if you take it on—is to introduce the process and form the habit. By putting "Daybook" first in your lesson plans, you will find more and more opportunities to say, "Open your Daybooks to the next blank page and date your entry." And you too may hear a muffled cheer and the admission to a neighbor: "I love it when we do these."

Back in the Real World

Though we are held to numerous time- and data-related measures in the current high-stakes-testing world of teaching, sometimes our best lessons don't hit home until much later. Teacher decision making should always revolve around what will help students be their best version of a human being. It is not always clear when something will take root. In the fall of the next year, a parent perks up when Daybooks are mentioned. Her daughter, Madison, who graduated three years earlier, is still using hers. The years following high school are tumultuous and rapidly changing, and Madison continued to rely on the habit of recording, observing, and sorting out those experiences. As a side benefit, her writing continues to grow. Daily writing is yet another tool to keep perspective on all that swirls around an emerging adult, but the daily habit also creates fluency in written thought.

A year after our course ended, I received this email from a very compliant student:

Hi Mrs. Tedrow,

It's Henry, one of your English students from spring of last year. I just wanted to reach out and say thank you for the idea of the daybook. I won't lie; I did not take the daybook very seriously when in your class. I thought of it as a hassle to write every day, not really seeing the point behind it. However, since entering college, I have begun keeping my own daybook. I try to write at least once every few days, and I find it gives me an outlet to confide in even on my roughest days.

. . . I just wanted to let you know of the impact you had on my life, one that stretches far outside the classroom. I hope to write for the rest of my life, and I thank you for getting me started on this journey. . . .

Building Buy-In: Steps, Lessons, and Routines

The following directions are presented in chronological order. The Daybook is introduced in gradual **steps**, each taking as much time as is needed. Along the way specific **lessons** are introduced to teach students ideas and theory that support reading, writing, and thinking. Finally, classroom **routines** are put in place to manage and collect the individualized work of the students.

Start with Yourself

If change is to occur, the first person in the room who must shift is the teacher. Establishing routines means changing *ourselves* first. But it's not hard to start forming the habit now—today. Go to your favorite source for school supplies and purchase a Daybook just for you. Indulge yourself. Find a book that speaks to you and claim it as your own—a space to vent, rant, dream, scribble, draw, make lists, and reflect on experience, on your teaching, on your future goals. Selfishly, use it to record all the business of your teaching life. When students write, take the time to write with them—first to share your writing in all its messiness with students, and then to make sense of the intense interactions of a teaching day. A teacher who writes with their students is a teacher who understands the challenges in getting words right. A teacher who participates in her own assignments also has a clear understanding of the ways in which an assignment can head down the wrong path or develop unexpectedly. Coaches of sports have played the game first and can offer reliable tips for improvement. Get in there and run the drills with students. You'll be better able to help them.

The best way to form a new habit is to *just get started*. Follow through the steps outlined to get both you and your classes going, and then experiment with writing as you go through the curricular year. Remember the Daybook when you make your plans. Employ good teaching decisions about what to add to the student-created text. Despite our need to have workable advance plans, this is a place where simply knowing that your students need to write will lead to exploring avenues to help them do just that. Absent any other plan, work a "stop and think in writing" pause into nearly every lesson, followed with lots of sharing of ideas. Additionally, your routine will provide students with valuable time to absorb and apply lessons. Before you know it, you and your students will be writing volumes.

Step One: Introduce the Daybook Requirement Along With Course Expectations

Plan to spend a good twenty minutes of class time talking to students about the requirement of having a Daybook of their own to bring to class. To prepare for this chat, I collect a variety of notebooks from area retailers and do my own investigating to direct students to local stores with a wide variety of notebooks in a range of prices. Some office supply stores have entire walls devoted to unique journals. It's a great place to stand and wait for the journals to start speaking. Other general merchandise stores routinely place notebooks on sale that can be found as cheaply as fifty cents. I frequent these and watch for back-to-school sales so there is always a pile of extra notebooks stored in the room.

Emphasize that the student can spend as much or as little on the book as they choose, but that they must find a book that *speaks to them*. And what does the book say? It says: "Write in me. You know you want to."

The focus for the first-day-of-class Daybook mini-lesson is to emphasize *finding the right book*, not what it is or how it is used. The students are only told that they will be expected to write in the book daily and should shop with an eye to finding something that matches their style and preferences. *What will make you want to write?* is the determining question.

Another feature of the chat on school supplies is finding the right writing utensil. Students consider: What's your favorite pen? Do you prefer pens or pencils when you get to choose? Lined or unlined paper? Are you a doodler? I first confess to my enduring love of shopping for school supplies. All those blank pages look like a literal clean slate and the hope that "this year might be different. No mistakes have been made yet, and my future is currently a blank page." Generally, my confession flushes out the school supply nerds, and a lively discussion encourages those enthusiasts to wax poetic on finding just the right tool to make schoolwork individual and enjoyable. One year we even formed our own gang: the Paper/Scissors Gang where entry was contingent on scoring a cool school supply.

Why Spend So Much Time Describing the Book?

Helping students identify their idiosyncratic writing process is one of the objectives of the Daybook, so spending time on the physical requirements for creative process is not frivolous. Defining a personal heuristic for how their creative process works becomes a reflective activity as the course proceeds. I want students to think about how their choices influence their motivation to write.

 Teacher Tip

Show the class the student-created dramatization available on YouTube of Taylor Mali's poem "On Girls Lending Pens" to get a discussion of school supplies going. This humorous poem also sends the subtle message that even the most mundane can be the topic of a writing piece.

Here is my criteria for a Daybook:

◆ Must make you want to write!
◆ Must be 5 × 7 or larger.
◆ Must be portable so it can be carried at all times.
◆ Can be lined or unlined—your choice.
◆ Spend as much or as little as you like.
◆ Number every page.
◆ Make it your own. Some students add art to the cover. Some collect artifacts.

The final directive is an early homework assignment to number every page.

At this point I model how I have numbered all the pages of my current, unsullied notebook, the one I will use along with my students throughout the term. Pages are numbered like a book, front and back on either the top or bottom right and left-hand outside corners. I, too, have purchased a distinctive

Figure 2.1 Some of the journals from my collection.

notebook for the express purpose of writing with my students as we go through the term. I also share previous Daybooks from my stack of them so they can see that it isn't hard to do a lot of writing in a term (Figure 2.1).

Finally, set a due date for bringing the Daybook and a favorite pen or pencil to class. Until your due date arrives, remind students daily that they need the Daybook because we are going to get started writing on that day.

Routine: Number All the Pages

The Daybook is intended to be exclusively reserved for student thoughts and explorations in writing. Numbering the pages has a surprisingly positive effect on helping students preserve this book for that exploration. Pages do not get torn out and used for other classes. In addition, the page numbers are very helpful in creating an organizing index in the back or a Table of Contents in the front. I use the back as an index. When students write continuously over time about a topic, they can flip to the back page and list the topic and all the pages where this topic appears in their book. Writers write about what engages their minds, responding to the world around them. The Daybook is a place for brainstorming on topics that attract our students' interest. Numbering pages helps students keep track of their evolving viewpoints on individual topics. Figure 2.2 is an example of the index from one of my recent Daybooks.

For teachers who have tried to use journals in the past but were unable to take them beyond a daily writing activity which went nowhere, the page number is the organizational feature that tracks writing for later use. For instance, when I plan a writing assignment, several prewrites or brainstorms are built into the process. By showing students how to index those writings on the last page, students can see how they are building their thinking around an assignment to come. In senior English, all students write a Personal Statement early in the course. This assignment is useful for post–high school plans like college or work applications. Before they write the first draft we do several Daybook entries to collect thinking about the values, skills, and talents they possess (see page 124 for these specific prompts). After the first entry for this assignment, I model how to start building an index on the last page of the Daybook. They title the index entry "Personal Statement" and then begin to record the pages where they have written about themselves. Later these can be accessed for the first draft. This has proven to be the most expedient and easiest way to make sense of continual writing.

Another organizing feature is to reserve some back pages of the journal for ongoing lists like "movies I want to see" or "books to read" as they are

Figure 2.2 A sample index page from the author's Daybook.

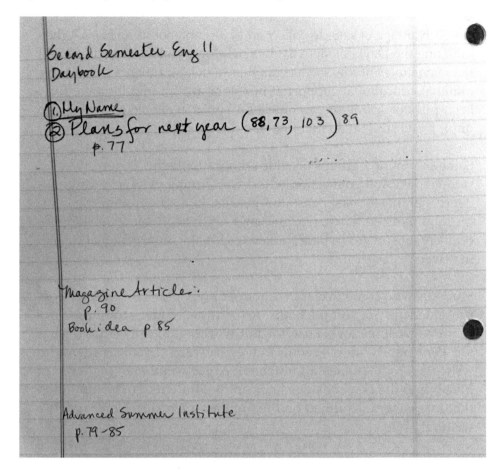

discussed by friends, seen as advertisements or in reviews, or picked up in classes. I show my lists to the students, modeling how learning goes on long after formal schooling ends.

Still another feature of the back pages can include an "About the Author" page (see Appendix B). In a writing class, this blurb would feature the influences on student writing. My students share their third-person blurbs at their first peer writing group meeting as an icebreaker. Content teachers can adapt the About the Author page to reflect their discipline. For a history class, one might include the author's *place in history* or a brief *bio-graphical* overview, perhaps to include any ancestral or cultural influences. In science, students can include "experiments that shaped my life" or in math they can write a short math biography of the student's history with number literacy.

✓ Teacher Tips

Take advantage of sales to collect and keep notebooks on hand. When initiating the Daybook activity, it is helpful for all students to start at the same time. For low socio-economic students, students who receive minimal educational support at home, or are chronically forgetful, I keep piles of spiral and composition books available to hand to an unprepared student on that first day.

Some community groups provide school supplies to underprivileged students. Form a connection with these groups to supply your students with notebooks, pens, and pencils. In a school with over 50% free and reduced lunch, our guidance office keeps stores of supplies on shelves in an area where students can make some personal choices in privacy.

Students who come to class without a Daybook when an activity is presented are not "off the hook" for writing. In fact, students in my room never have an excuse for not working. Supplies of all sorts are kept handy so everyone moves forward. Direct students to write on a regular sheet of notebook paper and then either tape or glue it into the Daybook at a later point. Students can be reminded that assessment is hinged on the number of entries. Don't lose the writing!

Step Two: Launching the Daybook—First Entries

The day has finally arrived, after much anticipation, when the students will get to use the Daybook in class. The lessons described below consume two entire ninety-minute block periods. Students value what we spend time on, and I want them to value the daily writing habit and see it as integral to an understanding of the course. I take as long as is needed to help students set a purpose for daily writing. After the lessons, all the students should have set a personal purpose for using the Daybook as well as a clear understanding of how the book will function in their learning life.

Back in the Real World

Bob Greene published the diary of his junior year in the book *Be True to Your School* in 1988. In 1964, Greene was a high school student in Bexley, Ohio—a suburb of Columbus. Even then he knew he wanted to be a writer. He challenged himself to keep a daily journal, and *Be True to Your School* is the publication of that diary. Greene worked as an award-winning columnist for the *Chicago Tribune* for twenty-four years and the record of his junior year in high school became a best seller. There is much in this book that a junior from the twenty-first century will relate to, and Greene keeps *nothing* back. Consider this book as fodder for how student writing might serve their understanding of themselves at a later age.

Lesson: Madman, Architect, Carpenter, Judge

Introduce students to the four characters who inhabit their mental lives. These characters are outlined in Betty S. Flowers's essay "Madman, Architect, Carpenter, Judge: Roles and the Writing Process" (1981). Over the years, it is clear that these roles resonate with students. The characters speak directly to what most students have already experienced in the writing process. Though non-English teachers may see these characters as tools only for composition, they are representative of a creative process used to advance any discipline. Inventions, the impact of history on our current world, and understanding of the physical world have all sprung from the human creative process.

Once students meet the characters (Figure 2.3) they become a part of our classroom discourse. Students often refer to them when discussing the phases of their own writing, as in, "I wrote this in my madman phase," when reflecting on writing assignments.

In our class, students return to the madman writings and collections of thought amassed in the Daybook to complete a personal writing piece of writing of their own. It's the "non-assignment assignment." For at least two writings, I will not direct the form the writing needs to take, nor will I provide a topic. Students create something from nothing and learn

Figure 2.3 A cartoon image of the four processes imagined as characters by Lars Eidsness.

about their own creative process. The madman writings will also give rise to required academic papers throughout the term. Disciplinary writing should also embrace madman writing as a method for attempting an understanding of content.

To introduce the writing process and the role of daily writing in that process, I write the names of the characters on the board explaining how they affect writing. I begin with the last and most familiar character to every student: The Judge.

Here is what I tell the students: "This little guy is the voice in your head who interrupts your writing. He tells you 'That's not good enough. You spelled that wrong. This is a dumb idea. No one will want to read that.' He needs to be shut down right away." The students usually nod their heads. They have met this character before (and he is us). I tell them how the author Anne Lamott, in *Bird by Bird* (1994), takes her critic and puts him in a mason jar and screws the lid on, tight. Only then is she freed to write. I share how other creators (artists, musicians) have told me that these characters work for them in their process as well. At some time in the creative process all artists must shut the inner judge down. Even a scientist, historian, or mathematician will find new creative methods to explore if they can tap into the inner madman.

Back in the Real World

The Goo Goo Dolls lead singer/songwriter John Rzeznik recently commented on his struggle with writer's block. He felt his early songwriting success limited his creative process. "You lose the ability to take the risk if you worry about the outcome," Rzeznik said. In the Daybook, the outcome doesn't matter. It is a space to relieve students of the pressure of an evaluation and free them to explore and celebrate their own creativity.

Then the students meet the other characters. Here is how I describe each one:

The Madman: "This creative character won't follow any of the rules. He takes chances. Tries things out. Writes down the side of the page. Writes upside down. Scribbles quickly, doodles, or stops in mid-thought. He doesn't stop to make corrections. Though far from mentally unstable, this fellow is uncensored creativity. It's your inner kindergartener; the fun person you were before school made you behave."

The Architect: "Bring this character in when you are ready to work with one of your off-the-wall madman scribblings. An architect makes plans and gives shape to a building. Would this writing be best as a letter to the editor? A short story? A poem? Maybe your band can use these words for lyrics. Maybe you are developing your thinking around relationships. Should you send some of your thoughts to your girlfriend, boyfriend, mother, or father in a letter? The architect helps the writing take shape. She considers the shape and size of the writing and who will be looking at it."

The Carpenter: "*Somebody* has to do the careful work of following the plan and nailing down every board." I tell my students that the boards are the sentences and the paragraphs. "Steal the best sentences and images from your madman and fill in the rest as you go."

Of course, I explain to the students, these stages are recursive. "In other words, as writers, we sometimes leap from the carpenter back to the madman, change formats in the architect phase, and then go back to the carpenter, and so forth while going through successive drafts. The writer knows she has arrived at a final draft when she feels she has exhausted the process and has nothing more to say.

"*Then* you can let in the judge, that mean internal English teacher, who can make sure that the writing is ready to be read by a wider audience. Or you can enlist friends and parents in helping to judge the work for those corrections that would have stopped you in your tracks early in the process."

Routine: Protecting Student Voice

Once students understand the roles, I tell them the Daybook is a place for their madman writing. It is a place to capture first thinking, not final draft thinking. These are "down drafts." It is the place to get thinking down on paper. And these drafts can take any form necessary because the writing is for them alone. Though it is a class assignment, I pinky-swear that I will not read their writing unless invited. This is writing for them—a place to experiment, a place to take risks. A place to try and fail and a place to succeed beyond their wildest dreams. The only thing I am concerned with is how often they are writing, and a daily entry is the goal, but other than that, there will be no mean Judge sitting on their shoulder. I tell my students, "If you write it down and you don't like it, don't use it. Turn the page and try something else. Forgive yourself. Move on. Make the editor get out of your head."

Teacher Tip

Extend the lesson by having students draw a picture of their internal judge. To emphasize that Daybook writing is not to be judged as good, bad, or indifferent, students can ceremoniously put their judges in a locked box, a mason jar, through a shredder, or dispose of them in another way.

Because the writing is responsive and off the top of the head, they are directed to do two things with the Daybook right away. Emphasize the importance of the first steps by providing the time in class:

◆ Inside the front cover, they should write "If this book is found, please return it to": and then complete it with contact information, including a phone number. I caution students that personal writing should not be left around because it is our rawest thoughts, and we generally do not want others to see this unfiltered thinking. I explain that I lost one of these notebooks in school and have never found it. I still wonder what I had written on those pages. Would anyone be offended? Be sure to get your contact information inside the front cover.

◆ Second, they are to skip the first page. A blank page when the book falls open will keep the book uninteresting to outside readers.

By the time I am finished inviting students into the writer's world, the classroom is buzzing with chatter about how they plan to write in the book. There is laughter and some sense of relief. This is writing that might be fun.

Step Three: Reviewing Daily Writing Expectations

Students are given the handout on "The Writer's Daybook," and I go over it, answering any questions. I want everyone to understand the purpose of the assignment (Figure 2.4). Though there are some rules to maintaining the notebook, these outlines just form a method for keeping track of very individual thinking. My objectives—to learn to make meaning, to practice, to develop a process, and to live like a writer—are overtly shared. I bring them in on the reasons for writing so they will see the benefits that extend beyond a grade.

Figure 2.4 The student handout for the Daybook assignment.

The Writer's Daybook
"Never a day without a line . . ."

"Close the door. Write with no one looking over your shoulder. Don't try to figure out what other people want to hear from you; figure out what you have to say. It's the one and only thing you have to offer."

—Barbara Kingsolver

Purpose: The purpose of daily writing is multiple:
- o   To gain a sense of yourself as a maker of meaning—a writer.
- o   To figure out a personal process that works for you.
- o   Daily writing helps you "read" the world as a writer.
- o   The Daybook is intended to help you create a thoughtful, deliberate purpose, to live with an idea over time, and ultimately follow it through to publication.
- o   If you live as a writer, you will read text as a writer, noticing structure and word choice.

The Daybook is a place to keep your thoughts. Writing serves many purposes, both formal and informal. This Daybook is a place to write down what makes you angry, sad, amazed . . . . Write down what you noticed and don't want to forget . . . . Record your reactions . . . . Live like a writer . . . .

What it is not: Not a diary. Not a journal. Not: what did I do today? But: what did I notice or think about today?

Guidelines:
- Do not use a heading . . . just the date.
- Never rip out pages!
- Write on the front/back of each page.
- Number the pages.
- Write legibly, but not your neatest handwriting.
- Use paragraph structure even as you draft. Form the habit of switching to a new paragraph when you introduce a new idea.
- Follow the rules of grammar and spelling, but not to the point that you lose the essence of what you're trying to write.
- Care for your notebook.
- Vary your topics.
- Make sure there is evidence of learning and risk taking in your notebook.
- Write a page—or 300 words—daily—in addition to our writing in class.

How on earth will you keep up with this?
Keep your notebook with you so you can write at **any place and time.** Pull out your writer's notebook when you have a few minutes with nothing else to do. The notebook should reflect you. If you like to draw, draw in your notebook. If you make lots of lists, then list away! You might also consider reserving a portion of your Daybook for artifacts like ticket stubs, photos, pressed flowers, etc.

Remember: WRITING CAN BE FUN!
Your notebook is a place to enjoy writing.

Step Four: Setting an Individual Purpose

So why write? Kelly Gallagher's "Big Eight Purposes for Writing" from his book *Teaching Adolescent Writers* (2006) hang in my classroom as our "Writing Reasons." They now become part of the rationale for students to commit to the daily writing. Students are instructed to turn to page three, date their entry, and record each reason for writing. The reasons to write, according the Kelly Gallagher, are:

> Writing is hard but "hard" is rewarding; Writing helps you sort things out; Writing makes you smarter; Writing helps to persuade others; Writing makes you a better reader; Writing helps get you into and through college; Writing helps to fight oppression; Writing prepares you for the world of work.
>
> (Gallagher 2006, pp. 16–21)

Lesson: Why Spend Energy Writing?

As I go over the reasons, students list them on page three of the Daybook, and I expand on them by using a combination of my personal experiences and evidence from the outside world. I want to suggest to them some reasons they might want to use their Daybook for their own purposes.

Gallagher's Reasons (2006):

1. **Writing is hard but "hard" is rewarding**. I tell them that everyone feels great achievement after setting a goal and then working hard to meet it. Getting our thoughts just right takes time and effort. Producing writing that meets our expectations is very rewarding. Students who have never attempted to create something entirely from their own ideas have the mistaken impression that good writing just happens, and you are either a good writer or you are not. As they work to get their messages in a form to satisfy their own expressive needs, they will soon see that creating a product can be a long process. But if they are writing regularly, and if we are prompting their thinking about serious, important topics through writing, they will sometimes be lucky enough to have the pen or computer handy when the muse strikes and an idea arrives, fully formed.

2. **Writing helps you sort things out**. For most students, this is a compelling reason to write. Life comes at us in a rush. Sometimes we need to slow down and take stock. Reflecting on our experiences helps us make sense of them. In their vulnerable developmental

years, the act of writing daily can help students absorb experiences and their learning. Writing helps to make sense of this blur of events. For the seniors, I encourage them to take this opportunity to mine this transitional year in their lives for opportunities to reflect on and figure out who they are, what they want to be, and to collect the inevitable successes and disappointments as they negotiate the last year of required education. Most memorable for the students is my own personal story (see page 34) of how writing resolved a major issue in my life and had done so in the lives of others.

3. **Writing makes you smarter**. There is a lot of research about how we can grow our intelligence and get better at things in general. In 1977 Janet Emig recognized writing as a unique form of thinking. This is where writing can help our students understand our instruction in the content areas. The act of writing is first and foremost an *act*, one that demands that students process what has been taught. Writing requires that we represent our thinking in an organized, symbolic manner. The action of writing both externalizes and personalizes instruction. Writing is a literal path to growing our brains. In addition, the more we write, the better writers we become. Like a sport, expertise comes through practice. One thing all writers have in common is that they write, regularly. "Butts in the chair," is how some writers express the necessity to be ready and writing when inspiration arrives. Writers also read differently. If you know you will write daily, you begin to look at your reading and your experiences as potential topics and genres. Daily writing helps students live life as writers: observing, recording, reflecting. And the very act of writing leads to more thinking and discovering. Sometimes you end up far away from where you started.

Back in the Real World

Recent research indicates that students can gain the most out of processing information and experiences while writing by hand rather than employing a computer. An argument can be made that there is still a place for the old technology of paper and pen or pencil. The study conducted by Pam A. Mueller and Daniel M. Oppenheimer found that students who take notes by longhand do better than students who use a laptop (2014). The slower act of handwriting seems to employ more processing of ideas to summarize experience.

4. **Writing helps to persuade others**. In a democratic society, we are lucky enough to be permitted to express an opinion, *but* we often won't get what we want or need unless we can make a compelling argument. Improved writing skills can land that job, convince a friend to become a lover, sell products, earn respect, improve the world. Writing daily flexes the thinking and writing muscles.

5. **Writing helps get you into and through college**. This one seems obvious, but students don't often realize that it is the essay that differentiates them from other potential candidates and earns them a seat at university. Scholarship essays open doors to monetary support as well as placement in honors dorms and overseas programs. At the University of Virginia, the theater department has taken some of these very personal insights provided in the entrance essay and turned them into one-act plays. Being able to represent ourselves on paper puts flesh on the human being behind all the accolades and achievements listed on the resume. In addition, writing is an essential component to college work. Students who leave high school as confident writers are much better prepared for their undergraduate work.

6. **Writing helps to fight oppression**. Editorials, letters of complaint, invitations to work for social justice: these give voice to an underclass and can ensure fair treatment in the workplace, the neighborhood, and the community. Improved literacy for all students means that writing must be in their toolbox along with strong reading skills. We need to send students into the world armed with effective skills in self-expression and critical thinking.

7. **Writing prepares you for the world of work**. Whether students like to hear it or not, many surveys of businesses indicate that strong writing skills opens doors. Sometimes this is *the* skill that lands the job. Other times writing is the threshold skill that leads to promotion (The National Commission on Writing 2004).

8. **Writing makes you a better reader**. Reading and writing are mirror images of one another. As the student works in one literacy, it informs the other. Readers make better writers and writers are better, closer readers. When we try to craft a metaphor, we have better appreciation for the striking comparisons we read. When we read and write like historians, scientists, artists, or laborers we are better consumers of those disciplines. We notice more as we read, and we mimic what we read in our writing. Both practices should be included in every discipline.

As I go over the reasons, the students record them in their Daybooks. Then I show them what a Daybook might look like after they add their own personal touch. These days I use student Daybook pages I have collected—with permission—so students can see how the pages reflect the personality and thinking strategies of the user. Before that I used sample pages from the man who coined the term "Daybook," Don Murray. These pages are printed in Thomas Newkirk's *The Essential Don Murray* (2009). Murray felt that all writers needed a place to capture "first thoughts," and he termed his notebook a Daybook to reflect the daily use and the need to carry the tool with him always. Murray's Daybook pages include lots of lists, some drawings, and many, many plans for his ideal writing schedule. He also analyzes the pens he likes to use for writing. With the document camera, I project pages of my own Daybook so students can see my messy, recursive process. All these models give students permission to employ their own process with the assignment.

Back in the Real World

I share several stories with my students to bolster the argument that writing can benefit them in their lives beyond schooling. The sharing of personal stories by teachers goes a long way to building a community of trust in the classroom. Stories humanize teachers and create a climate that fosters the modeling of coping strategies for life's circumstances. So, I share. If you have stories which relate, I recommend sharing your own.

Writing Helps You Sort Things Out

Writing provides solace that goes beyond recording experiences. It can help writers process experience and heal trauma. Writing, in fact, is an essential tool in helping returning war veterans who suffer with post-traumatic stress disorder. If time allows, I share *The New York Times* article that explores how military veterans are encouraged to write out their wartime experiences (Simon 2013).

But probably the most compelling evidence comes from my own experience. When I was about the same age as my students, eighteen, my car was hit head-on by a drunk driver. Immediately following the accident, I had vivid dreams where I awoke trying to climb over the front seat of the car to get into the back before impact. In all the years following the accident, I often relived the memory of the crash as physical sensations when I drove at night. I imagined headlights crossing the centerline and smashing into my car. I could feel the impact again in my face and legs. I knew what it would feel like to be hit at thirty, or forty, or fifty miles per hour. When my own daughter came of driving age, I decided to explore my fears in writing and came as close as I possibly could to recreating the experience. Finally, I shared the writing with a group of peers in the summer institute of the Northern Virginia Writing Project. Though the experience of feeling the crash had persisted for over twenty-five years, after working on the writing I have never had a flashback since. In my own life, writing has had a healing effect.

Writing Gets You Into and Through College

I share several successes former students have had where their writing affected their ability to attend and pay for college. I share the $6,000 scholarship a student earned through a single essay developed in her writing group, or the variety of local scholarships won on the judgment of student essays. Others have won cameras or positions on college newspapers. Some have shared a portfolio of their written work completed in the Advanced Placement literature class to gain entrance to other writing-intensive courses. Some have even included published work in their resumes, which set them apart from their peers in going through the application process. These pieces, collected from students who took this route while in the classroom, are shared as evidence that our school assignments can sometimes reach a wider audience. Encouraging students to send writing out of the classroom for contests and publications has been a hallmark in my courses, begun through the continual effort to make English class as relevant and important as the journalism class. Students can see that writing has a tangible effect on their lives.

Lesson: Reading and Writing for Goal Setting

Next, I share two articles on setting goals. Though the purpose in reading the articles is a part of setting their own goals for the Daybook, I also use them to introduce the habit of annotating, an important writing-to-learn tool. The information also shapes goal setting within the context of the entire course that will be documented in their end-of-course portfolio. This time-out for reading serves three purposes in the curriculum. In a history, science, art, band, or math class, articles about important writers, thinkers, and change makers and their processes in meeting success would do the double duty of introducing habits of success along with content.

 Teacher Tip

The Daily Routines Blog (dailyroutines.typepad.com) is a collection of the processes of many artists, writers, and thinkers. Though the blog is no longer active, the information remains accessible. The creator of the blog, Mason Currey, pulled his collection into the 2013 book *Daily Rituals*. Both are a great source for discovering and modeling for students the processes of thinkers in many disciplines.

The articles are: "Why 3% of Harvard MBAs Make Ten Times as Much as the Other 97% Combined"

(http://sidsavara.com/personal-productivity/why-3-of-harvard-mbas-make-ten-times-as-much-as-the-other-97-combined) and "Getting Healthy: When Does Prediction Help People Change Their Habits?"

(www.sciencedaily.com/releases/2011/03/110317131043.htm).

The first of the short articles explains that successful Harvard graduates did one thing that their less successful counterparts did not do: they set and wrote down their goals. The second article provides evidence that a dieter's prediction of how well he or she might stick to changing eating habits is a predictable factor in whether the dieter will maintain the new habit. The students are to read to discover the two keys to success.

The Reading Assignment

Here is the assignment the students complete in class:

Read with this question in mind: What are the key strategies that can lead to achieving your own goals in life?

Read and mark as you go. Use a highlighter to mark passages that help you answer the purpose question. In the margins, pair the highlighted passages with a record of your thinking. Then, on a sheet of notebook paper, write an ABC paragraph to answer the above purpose question:

A   Answer the question.
B   Back it up by summarizing, paraphrasing, or quoting from the two articles.
C   Comment on the information you have presented in your answer. (Sum up, conclude, connect to your life.)

The ABC paragraphs and the marking of text are both habits encouraged in the Reading and Writing standards of the Common Core, and we are building these routines with these first articles early in the course. After writing the ABC paragraph, students share and discuss their findings at their tables. Finally, we discuss the recommendations as a class.

Lesson: Creating a Mission Statement

After reading and sharing, we complete the last step in goal setting for the Daybook: students write a **Mission Statement**. This will be their first true entry in the Daybook. The directions are simple. After taking into consideration the reasons to write and the tools for success, they must explain to themselves in writing their personal goals for the Daybook and make a prediction on how well they feel they might succeed in reaching the goal of daily writing.

> ### Back in the Real World
> The Mission Statement idea came from *Writing Tools: 50 Essential Strategies for Every Writer* by Roy Peter Clark (2006). Clark recommends a Mission Statement as a precursor to all types of writing as a method to pinpoint the overall message the writer intends to send a reader. This Mission Statement is tailored for the daily writing habit.
>
> Here is a sampling of Mission Statements students have shared with me.
>
> ◆ "I will use this daybook to my advantage, by writing in it at least once every day. Like Mrs. Tedrow once said, 'Writing makes you smarter,' and to hear that, I should have started writing everyday a long time ago." —Male, senior (class joker)
> ◆ "I plan to write down in here the contents floating down my stream of consciousness in order to decipher them later. Also, I plan on using this daybook as a tool to improve my writing in both length and literary value. I have been told before that writing is like a sport, the more you practice the better you get, so I will call this journal my practice field and off I go to put in the hours every day to become the best writer I can possibly become." —Male, senior (second-language learner)
> ◆ "I think I will write every day. It does not seem like I am doing homework. I am just expressing myself. Pouring out

my thoughts on paper clears my head. I am constantly analyzing things and have many things to say at the end of the
day." —Female, senior

◆ "I want to use my daily journal to get to know myself better
and to sort out emotions and problems that I'm facing. So
I'm basically using it as a therapy method. I'm also hoping
to improve my writing through this daily activity too." —
Female, senior (recently orphaned)

Step Five: Setting a Purpose for Learning in the Course

The night following the writing of the Mission Statement, the students are
required, as they will be every night, to fill a page with writing.

For this first assignment, I choose the topic for the nightly writing,
unlike most writing they will do outside the classroom. The students must
write in response to this question: *Why study literature?* The page of writing—although not read by me—will be their ticket into a discussion on
reading which sets the purpose for our course and study of the required
literature. As a part of classroom expectations, students are required to
have their Daybooks with them always, to form the habit of keeping an
accessible place for thinking. The tone for this expectation is set with the
first assignment.

Other curricular areas should consider asking students a similar *Why
are we learning this?* question for a first writing in a course. Asking students
to create their own purpose for learning not only sets the tone for inquiry
but also serves as an initial assessment of the knowledge and attitudes students bring to the table.

 Teacher Tip

An additional Daybook writing assignment is to add an "About the
Author" blurb to the inside back cover. As students create their personal "book," they are also learning about features of most books.
The About the Author assignment appears in Appendix B. It can be
adjusted to have a focus on the student's life as a historian, scientist,
artist, musician, or math genius.

Routine: Classroom Structures That Support Writing and Sharing

There are several routines put in place beginning with the very first writing. Following the routine helps establish writing time as sacred time in the classroom.

Students are instructed to **date every entry**. This establishes a timeline for them and a method of counting entries for me. Can they make more than one entry in a day? Certainly. If they write more than once, they should continue to date every entry, even if two or three entries carry the same date. One year, Carolyn, an aspiring songwriter, creative artist, and singer for an acoustic threesome, responded with enthusiasm to the Daybook assignment. When Carolyn turned in her Daybook to confirm the fifty-five entries we had tallied for the whole class, her entries ranged in the hundreds and the entire book was a work of art reflecting her skill as an artist as well as songwriter. She also shared a recording on CD of the song she wrote after using the Daybook to create the words and music. How would a teacher assess that? It is a happy moment when our schoolwork acknowledges and embraces a student's interests.

Writing time in the classroom is **quiet time**. Two routines help establish this personal thinking time. First: set a timer. If you think your students would benefit from seeing how much time is left, project a timer on your screen. However, a simple kitchen timer (I have many, all from dollar stores) will serve the timekeeping purpose. My favorite projected timer is from Toolbox pro (http://ideas.gstboces.org/programs/timer/). Students are told that the room must be quiet while the timer is running. If they've run out of ideas for writing they should honor the quiet time so all students can hear their own thinking; however, students should challenge themselves to write for the entire time, by simply following their thinking to see where it leads. It is *after* our first response to a prompt when the surprises in thinking often occur. Keep writing. The timer is key to classroom management.

Model the behavior: When students write, pull a desk around where all the students can see you and write. If you ask students to share, be prepared to occasionally share your writing as well.

 Teacher Tip

Warn students in advance if you expect them to share their writing. Let students know when writing will not be shared. This maintains the student's ability to self-edit the topics they are willing to share.

My daily writing routine goes something like this:

"Get out your Daybooks, turn to the next clean page, and date your entry. Today is . . ."

"Today we are going to write on . . ." (Or: "Today I'd like you to try . . ." "Today I'd like you to think about . . .")

"You will be sharing this writing with a partner so, if you have something you don't want to share, don't write it." Or: "This writing will not be shared. It is for your eyes only."

The purpose of the writing determines whether sharing will occur. Sometimes the writing is intended to spark a discussion. Those writings will be shared. Other times the writing is to develop a stance or to connect with a reading. Those writings are personal and written to the self. I do not expect those to be shared, although the opportunity is sometimes offered. All students get an opportunity to share with a partner. Later, pull the large group into discussion. "Let me hear your thinking." is an easy entry into large group sharing.

Finally, when writing is shared, tell the students to simply read what they wrote. Students (and adults) tend to want to talk *about* what they wrote. But having students read what they wrote serves two purposes. First, it is faster. Talking about writing tends to go off track. Second, the writer begins to hear his or her own written voice, as opposed to the speaking voice, one that can circle back on itself, is frequently interrupted by "haws" (um, like, you know), includes incomplete thoughts, and can be riddled with digressions. These reasons are not secret, so I tell students why they should *just read what you wrote*.

Sharing in the classroom is the first level of formative assessment. Listen for what students do or do not understand, but also listen with an ear to congratulate rather than to reprimand. Comments to students should be honest but positive. Work to find what the student is doing well and reward them for sharing by pointing out the strengths. This will encourage more sharing throughout the room and build the safe community you will need if you want students listening and sharing with each other. For those introverts who rarely share, giving them the opportunity to write their thoughts first means they are still able to participate in the discussion. The quiet think time means they won't have their ideas run over by the extroverts who tend to process thinking out loud. Even if students choose not to speak, they have a starting point to measure their thinking against others. The student sharing of a response invites all of us to rethink our own viewpoints, comparing them to another view.

For the students, sharing can motivate more writing. Rather than assigning a grade, the reading meets with a real and immediate audience, one that responds as a reader. (See page 142 for a distinction between reader and evaluator responses.) It also celebrates writing that has proven successful. Initial sharing is done with a partner or a group at a table. Later students are invited to read to the entire class voluntarily. Even better, a partner can nominate another student to read to the large group. The very act of nominating someone to share an interesting writing is a form of positive assessment. My prompts to the students are simple: "Take a minute to share with a partner." After everyone reads I say, "Would anyone like to share with the class?" or, if there is no one forthcoming, "Would anyone like to volunteer a partner to share with the class?" Another prompt which can elicit student sharing is to ask: "Did anyone find a good way to say this?" Or, "Did you hear someone else read something that you would recommend we all hear?" Another invitational prompt is, "Let me hear what you are thinking."

For some readings, students are invited to come to the front of the class and sit in the author's chair, which in my classroom is a brightly painted stool set front and center. Either way, from the desk or from the author's chair, sharing sends the message that we are all authors here, and we all have something to say. In the content area, responses to content-related prompts are immediate feedback for the teacher on student understanding. Misconstrued concepts can be retaught. Clear understandings can be rewarded. Hearing a content area concept in "student language" can be instructive for everyone else in the room.

Routine: Lather, Rinse, Repeat—Building a Habit in Twenty-One Days

These are the lessons that help my students determine the where, the how, and most importantly the *why* of daily writing. But as a partner in forming this new way of looking at writing, you are not ready to set them loose yet. As with all habits, we need reinforcement. I once heard that it takes twenty-one days of repetition to cement a new habit. So for the next three weeks the Daybook will be central to the beginning activities of the classroom. We use it every day. Later, when other plans intercede, I am not too worried if the Daybook doesn't quite fit into those plans. But in the beginning, the Daybook is front and center. I want to help my students see value and use in writing down their thoughts. I want to be a part of forming this habit of writing daily and using writing as a tool for figuring out and writing down what they feel they already know. I want them to recognize their own independent thinking and own those thoughts. As E. M. Forester is credited with saying, "How do I know what I think until

I see what I say?" Frequent writing and sharing helps students identify their own thoughts and process content material, all while hearing a written voice.

As we go through the course I keep track of how many entries students should have and which prompts I have used, marking some as particularly useful to student understanding of content or others as helpful for developing ideas or individual thinking.

Tallying the number of entries becomes important on the twenty-first day. I ask students on that day to perform a mini-audit of their Daybooks. This is a quick assessment and serves as a reminder to students that continual writing in our subject is a course requirement. It gives students a chance to evaluate themselves on how well they are keeping up with the task.

Note that this brief form (Figure 2.5) brings students in on the evaluation of the task (How many entries is good enough? How close are you to your stated goal?) without dictating a grade. Also, auditing the journal through the form honors the promise to let students have a risk-free space. I do not have to collect the journals, only the form. In both instances, it is implied that the responsibility for learning is the student's alone. I've found that students are very honest.

Though I assign a few completion points for the audit, I eagerly read them to see how students are progressing. Reminders to keep up with entries and short check-in conferences with individuals follow this brief assessment.

Figure 2.5 A sample mini-audit. This can be adjusted to reflect any questions that match your instructional needs.

Name: _____

Mini-Daybook Audit

You have been keeping a Daybook for 21 days. A good habit can be formed by repeating it for 21 straight days. If you have been "perfect" (and few of us are) you will have 30 entries. If you are less than perfect, then you will come close.

- How many entries would you consider "close enough" to forming a good habit? _____
- Count your entries. How many do you have? _____
- Find the first entry you wrote without my prompting. Count the words. How many words did you write? _____
- Count the last entry you wrote without my prompting. How many words did you write? _____
- Fluency, getting more words on paper in less time, is one Daybook goal. How are you doing?

  _____

- Read your Mission Statement. How close are you coming to your prediction?

  _____

Summing Up

It is tempting to dive into curriculum at the beginning of a year when the scope of the curriculum and the timeline are bearing down. But spending time establishing predictable routines, while building a purpose for learning, is time well spent. And our students learn to value what *we* spend time on. If you want them to value daily writing, emphasize it. Beyond learning content, students will be learning habits of mind that lead to success in their work to come. Providing routine also creates safety through predictability. Reliable routines also reduce classroom management issues. Later, you will find that these routines speed effectiveness in covering content.

For the Daybook, Incorporate the Following:

◆ Provide all students with a good start by spending time setting up the notebook, developing its purpose, and motivating students to find their own uses of daily writing.
◆ Keep supplies handy to bridge the supply gap for students who struggle.
◆ Number pages to reduce the need to micromanage the location of writings. Students can index later.
◆ Use the Daybook routinely in class.
  – Set a timer for the writing and instruct students this is quiet time that allows everyone to hear their own thoughts.
  – Plan for regular sharing. Ensure safety by warning students in advance that writing will be shared. Invite students in: "Would anyone like to share?" Or: "Let me hear your thinking." Reward students by commenting only where the student writing is successful.
  – Write with your students to better understand the process, model good writing behaviors, share occasionally with students, coach students in their writing, and fine tune your own assignments.
  – Enjoy the process.

The next chapter reviews the characteristics of questions which prompt the student thinking needed to develop understanding. The theory behind writing for learning is described.

3

What Will We Write About?

Understanding the Characteristics of Effective Prompting

"Writing is thinking. To write well is to think clearly. That's why it's so hard."

—David McCullough

What to Expect

This chapter explains how prompting provides opportunities for students to explore and consume ideas in their own language. Understanding what to expect from student writing and thinking requires a definition of question types and the general parameters for prompting that will inspire thoughtful, successful writing. Good prompting moves student writing from a potential dead end to an activity that serves both the students and the learning. This overview guides teachers in understanding the purpose of different question types so teachers can formulate questions that work within varied content.

Chapter Topics

- ◆ Defining the teacher's role in prompting student writing.
- ◆ Reviewing theory for writing as a tool for learning.
- ◆ Examining the types of questions and their relation to Bloom's taxonomy of thinking.
- ◆ Anticipating the types of answers questions will produce.
- ◆ Categorizing prompting around the patterns of intellectual behaviors practiced and inspired in students.

Thinking About Prompts: The Teacher's Role

An incident about ten years into my teaching career (see the *Back in the Real World* feature) clearly illustrated that my job as instructor needed to shift from assigning work to helping kids locate what they know so they can write clearly and cogently around our assigned products in the classroom. Or, as I saw it, my prompting needed to help kids prewrite, collect, and brainstorm about what they already know or think they have learned before asking them to write formally on any topic. If I were to see successful written products, I needed to teach students how to develop their ideas around the assigned work. Additionally, students needed lots and lots of time to write about what they know—usually through the lens of their own thoughts and experiences. All experience feeds into the development of argument and draws personal connections to literature, or science, or math, or history. I needed to help students locate those connections as they are immersed in new learning experiences. They also need frequent, ungraded opportunities to dabble in their thinking and to experiment with new vocabulary and concepts. They need to write lots of junk before they can be expected to develop worthy products. A single assignment was not going to bring out their best thinking.

This insight helped me to consider daily writing as a tool, not just for expression and fluency, but also to foster learning. With this goal in mind, I began to focus efforts on developing prompts and tools to engross students in their own thoughts, gently guided by the curriculum.

In the early days of journaling or the use of a writer's notebook, my prompting, and that of many teachers, centered on reviewing or responding to the day or selecting random spurs for writing. Teachers gravitate to books with titles like *180 Daily Writing Prompts* for ideas. Many of these are good for creative writing but are often not tied to what is going on in a course of study and are inappropriate if you are trying to *teach* through writing in the subject area. If the prompts are not tied to classroom use, and both teachers and students find little use for the writing, the initiative seems extraneous and withers on the vine. This was my early experience.

Back in the Real World

As an at-risk student, Joey fit the bill from the start. He arrived three weeks into the school year, transferring from another state. His adjustment was difficult. When he was present in the ninth grade English class, disruption followed. It was difficult to tell his skill level since most of his energy was devoted to avoiding schoolwork. He wrote, but only minimally. And his writing was rife with surface errors: a lack of punctuation, no capitalization, frequent spelling errors, all presented in horrible handwriting. His indifference was apparent on many levels.

One afternoon he arrived a stunning fifteen minutes late. He interrupted our silent writing to tell me about an altercation with an administrator in the hall. "We're writing," I whispered. "Sit down and write it out." He grabbed his notebook and moved to a far corner of the room, turned sideways in his chair, and began to write.

In a few minutes the class moved on to the lesson for the day. But Joey did not. He continued to write. In fact, he did none of the activities that day. He simply wrote for the remaining fifty-five minutes. I did not disrupt him since, for once, he was displaying incredible focus on his work.

When class ended, Joey was the last to get up and leave. He stopped in front of me on the way out the door and handed me the open journal. "Here," he demanded. "Read it." And then he left.

What I read that day astounded me. In three long pages of carefully written legible text, Joey had explained the entire altercation in the hallway, his role in it, and his anger at what he viewed as an injustice. And here's the part that *really struck* me: it was fluid. It was interesting. And it had dialogue. Properly punctuated and capitalized dialogue. With quotation marks and everything. It was a fine piece of narrative that included imagery, conflict, rising action, and a climactic moment. Besides learning that Joey had many skills he was choosing not to use, I was impressed with his storytelling talents.

I don't know how much I taught Joey that year. He was gone before school ended after many more altercations. But before leaving our school, Joey taught me an important lesson: most kids (and adults) can write well if they both know and care about what they are writing. Though hardly a model student, when presented with a task that he cared about, chose for himself, and had personal knowledge of, Joey was willing to focus a lot of effort (an entire class period and three handwritten pages) on reaching his own goal. Joey's example completely changed my view of the classroom. Too often, I realized, we ask students to write about subjects they are not equipped to discuss or have little interest in. Through this overreach, students produce awkward prose and come to believe that they cannot write at all, when that is far from the truth.

The Daybook, defined as a tool to collect *thinking*, frees teachers to use prompting to achieve several goals for students and the course. Once committed to the idea that student thinking and writing improves if there is a place to regularly visit the inner life for a clearer understanding of content, prompting becomes more focused and the usefulness of the writings is immediate and apparent to all. Rather than writing for the sake of writing, which has its own reasoning and is still possible in an outside-the-class assignment to write daily to process life events, much of the in-class writing is directed toward developing understanding around the course—with an occasional veer into the realm of writing creatively for the sheer joy of seeing what we can do with words and for manipulating and working with course vocabulary and concepts.

In the case of the English classroom, the instructional focus is on analyzing and responding to the writer's craft while developing our own craft. Many prompts focus on trying out what we see authors doing. In the content area, Daybook writing should focus on the essential questions of any given curriculum. Asking each day, "What do students need to know in this unit or in this lesson?" can help frame the prompting for a content area class.

The goal for all prompting is to help students form very personalized connections to curriculum and to express that understanding first in their own language, the language they learned at home from mom and dad and which is nearest to their speech. I call this strategy "providing as many doors and windows as possible for students to climb through and enter a concept."

Looking at Theory: What to Expect in Student Response

James Britton, a researcher in composition in the 1970s, recognized the importance of expressive writing—writing which is closest to the speech of the individual—as the important first step in understanding and processing ideas. He identified expressive writing as the matrix through which all other writing must first move ("The Composing Process and the Functions of Writing," 1978). Students need to literally put new ideas in their own words before they can understand them.

Prompting this kind of writing, writing which students always characterize as "easy," helps students process learning while permitting a wrestling with ideas at a very individual level. After seeing what they know, students more easily transform what is said informally into either informational texts, like reports or essays—what Britton refers to as transactional writing—or into an artistic form like a narrative or poem (see Figure 3.1). In addition to helping students understand their learning, expressive writing builds fluency—the ability to freely write without the anxiety and fear most students connect with the writing task. As students generate more writing, their confidence builds and the anxiety associated with most writing falls away. It is, indeed, easy to write in this form.

Skipping the first step of expressing oneself in the accessible language of speech is common in most content areas and results in prose that is a tangled mess. Teachers exclaim, "These kids can't write!" when what is truer is that *these kids* have not been permitted time to think within the content. Had they found their thoughts first and then moved on to the formal product, the result would have more clarity. By the time some students reach secondary school, their lack of practice in expressing ideas has been compounded by years of neglect. Students need to reach a level of *fluency*, a state in which thoughts flow easily and fearlessly onto the page. As Joey revealed (see the *Back in the Real World* feature), when given the chance, some of our least likely students can surprise us with sudden clarity around ideas they clearly own. In responses to in-class prompts, teachers should expect language that sounds very similar to speech, always in the voice of the student writer, and depending on the student's home language, often not in standard English. When looking at expressive text, it is important to focus on the ideas expressed and not the form. Students will avoid writing freely and fluently if prompt responses are subjected to close grammatical scrutiny. Put the red pen away for these practice runs. We want to make student thought visible by capturing the inner monologue that goes on. Collecting in a Daybook holds thinking, not correctness.

Figure 3.1 Function categories.

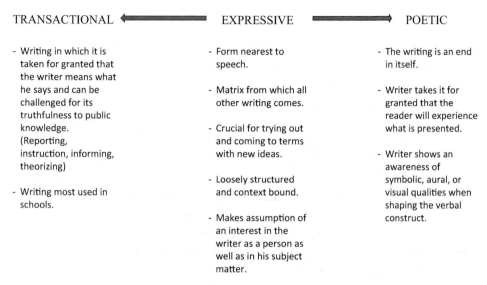

TRANSACTIONAL ⇐══════	EXPRESSIVE ══════⇒	POETIC
- Writing in which it is taken for granted that the writer means what he says and can be challenged for its truthfulness to public knowledge. (Reporting, instruction, informing, theorizing)	- Form nearest to speech.	- The writing is an end in itself.
	- Matrix from which all other writing comes.	- Writer takes it for granted that the reader will experience what is presented.
	- Crucial for trying out and coming to terms with new ideas.	
		- Writer shows an awareness of symbolic, aural, or visual qualities when shaping the verbal construct.
- Writing most used in schools.	- Loosely structured and context bound.	
	- Makes assumption of an interest in the writer as a person as well as in his subject matter.	

Source: From James Britton, *The Development of Writing Abilities*, Macmillan Co., 1975.

James Britton described three functions of writing in 1975 (see Figure 3.1). The center function, expressive, is most often ignored in schooling, though students find this the easiest to access. It is a first, necessary step in creating other forms of writing.

If we process through speech, then why not just talk about ideas? This is a legitimate question. If students need to put their ideas in their own words, why not just provide a prompt and let them talk? Currently, this parallels the turn-and-talk strategy in use in many classrooms. But writing first is important. The work of Janet Emig (1977) reveals that writing is an entirely separate form of thinking and her observations have been supported by more recent brain research and work with victims of trauma. The act of writing is both a mental and physical process that requires the transformation of thinking into symbolic language. It appears that this process of combining both mental and physical activity simultaneously clarifies and cements learning (Emig 1977; Mueller and Oppenheimer 2014; Karpicke and Blunt 2011). It is also highly individual and active. Students cannot passively let the talking of their fellow students—or their teachers—wash over them. They must get in there and *make the meaning* for themselves first. Stopping and writing is time well spent in the classroom. In my opinion, the turn-and-talk strategy should be amended to write, then turn and talk. An additional advantage to writing before talking is gained by the introverted student who cannot process orally as well as the extroverted student. Slowing down by writing first lets the less verbally inclined student have the chance to process learning before another more aggressive student does the processing for them. In this way, a short stop-and-write is highly individualized for every student in the room.

Finally, a content area teacher might assume that an English teacher could instruct their students in how to use expressive writing in English class and students would then naturally transfer that skill to their other studies, relieving the content teacher of the need to employ the writing in their course and to just get on with the task of presenting new information. Unfortunately, this kind of transfer does not appear to happen. The critical thinking that expressive writing engenders must be done in the context of the new information. Students need the opportunity to think critically in every subject. Daniel Willingham maintains that "thinking is combining information in new ways" (2009, p. 8). The opportunity to think—and subsequently own the new knowledge—comes from the chance to combine new information with experience. But the idea that critical thinking skills are transferrable—that you can learn the process of thinking in English class and thus apply it to history—is false. Students need to practice thinking within the context of a subject, and not just once, but repeatedly. Critical thinking processes must be tied to the background knowledge provided in each discipline. Willingham suggests that the background knowledge be provided first before introducing an item of curiosity that students could tie to the new background knowledge. Writing that engenders thought, therefore, must be integrated into every content. Not until about the age of twenty-five, according to Willingham (2009), will critical thinking skills transfer across disciplines.

Structuring Prompts: The Importance of Choice, Personal Connection, and Utility

> The basic idea is a simple one: when an audience is safe you put out words more easily, when it is dangerous you find it harder. . . . [A] dangerous audience can inhibit not only the quantity of your words but also their quality.
>
> —Peter Elbow, *Writing With Power*

The prompts which most effectively allow students a way in to new content offer the latitude for student choice in the phrasing of the response and an availability of choice in the prompted topics. This can be achieved through prompts that first generate lists students can select from (my version of open doors and windows). These prompts start *Make a list of the* . . . . Or the prompt itself may inspire choice because it is wide enough to allow a student to review experiences from both in or outside the classroom that parallel the category or concept presented. Some of these prompts begin *Think of a time when . . . .* Another powerful prompt is to ask students *What do you notice?*

It is easy to see when a prompt works for expressive writing. Students jump on it, hardly realizing that they are writing. Primarily, they feel they are responding to an interesting idea or situation. The writing is secondary. Another component that makes the writing "easy" is its low-risk nature. There is hardly any way to respond incorrectly since most prompts rely on the truth of the student experience, and every student senses this. Finally, if the writing is immediately referenced through sharing and discussion, its creation is relevant to both the student and his learning. Choosing prompts which fit with the flow of the class integrates writing seamlessly into the course work.

When given the opportunity for choice, students choose well, favoring activities that are just within the realm of a challenge they are ready to tackle. Though the choice varies from student to student, it often succeeds in revealing a clear student voice—a reference again to capturing written speech. The act of choosing means that students *will* succeed, so prompts that allow this work best. When students choose, they also create the situation that Daniel Willingham describes as a zone where there is just enough challenge to make the task interesting while still holding out the probability of high success. Willingham says that people "enjoy mental activity" (4) *if* there is a hope of success. If you are of the opinion that educators must "trick" students into thinking, then you are exactly right. Writing from personal experience has the right mix of fun and challenge that tricks students into doing the thinking you are hoping to generate. The best prompts present a problem that allows accessible success. Through their own reflections and remarks, students clearly feel pleasure after many of these activities. The opportunity to choose means that success is within their power.

In the content area, careful prompting allows students to show us what they *do know* instead of emphasizing what they *do not know*. Traditional tests are vehicles for teasing out what students didn't get. Writing prompts are opportunities for all students to display what they did get, then share it with a partner, and gain from a reciprocal interaction: I share what I know. You share what you know. When it is all in "kid language," everybody has another opportunity to hear content reframed in a potentially accessible form. When responses are shared, the writing has an immediate, course-related use and cries of "Will this be graded?" tend to disappear.

Developing Prompts: Toward an Understanding of Questions That Produce Useful Products

Okay. So you've decided to incorporate the prompting of writing in a risk-free space, the Daybook, for your students. How do you go about creating or finding these prompts?

Have a Plan for the Writing—and Let Your Students in on It

Sometimes a prompt response will be used for sharing. Students should be told in advance of the writing if you expect to have them share with others. We all have an editor in our heads, and if we know we are going to share writing, we may quickly switch topics or our method of writing. This is an important first choice for the writer: how much am I willing to risk with this audience and this writing?

Other prompts are intended as fodder for discussion. Students should also be aware of this. By simply saying, "Think in writing for a few minutes before we discuss this as a class," you help students understand the purpose of the writing.

Finally, some topics can be so deeply personal that students need to be given a safe space to take a risk. After giving a prompt of this nature let students know that "this writing is just for you, and I do not expect you to share unless you choose to." Students need an opportunity to take risks if they are going to grow, but how and when to share risky writing with others must be a choice on the part of the student. The directive from you is also a subtle reminder that public writing is adjusted to audience. What students write for each other differs from what they write only for themselves and is even more dramatically different from what they write for "us"—academia.

Understanding What to Expect From Questioning

Before delving into the chapters on more specific prompting, an understanding of questioning can help when devising prompts for a subject area.

Questions come in differing levels that correspond to Bloom's taxonomy of thinking, which begins with the lowest level of recall and moves onto the higher levels of comprehension, application, analysis, synthesis, and evaluation. In various resources the questions are defined as Level 1, Level 2, and Level 3 questions. Students should be taught the levels too, but teachers should keep these in mind when developing content-related questions as writing prompts. Test your question against the levels to be sure students will be able to construct a useful response.

Level 1 questions are merely questions which recall a fact or detail. (*What is the commutative property in math?*) The answers will be brief, since there is a factor of correctness to the answer. Though recall is low on the ladder of Bloom's taxonomy, do not dismiss these questions entirely. Having students define terms or concepts in their own language can be extremely helpful in owning the material. Divergent thinking and exploration come from the higher-level questions.

Level 2 questions ask students to draw an inference—a kind of inductive reasoning. Some of these questions can be used to inspire writing that combines student experience and thought with content. Level 2 questions can also be used to engender curiosity. ("What might cause a flame to turn blue when heating a metal? Write as many explanations as are possible.") Looking back over what you know and combining it with what you are unsure of is highly motivating. Human beings are innately curious and our chance to observe can inspire questions that help students find a reason to want to learn. Using our intuitive powers can drive curiosity around a new subject. Additionally, these questions provide an opportunity to *infer*, a muscular intellectual tool.

Level 3 questions inspire discussions and lead students into a "what if" frame of mind. ("Now that you know what displacement is, how could this property drive an invention?") We can synthesize what we have been exposed to and create new knowledge and ideas with the right kinds of questions. This is true application of learning and speaks to the creator in all of us. All students should get the opportunity to play with and extend the concepts they understand. Level 3 questions have lots of possible answers and are rich drivers of discussion.

When designing a prompt, keep in mind your objectives and the level of thinking you are hoping to engage with students. Level 3 questions—or open-ended questions—will inspire the widest range of thought. These often begin with "why," "what," or "how."

Teacher Tip

Once you are committed to prompting student thinking, you will begin to see potential topics and prompts everywhere you look. In Appendix A is a listing of sources for prompts in books, websites, and even in apps.

Categorizing Prompts: Recognize the Intellectual Behavior in Practice

In a review of the writing my students have done over the years, I find that prompting falls into four main categories, with some of the prompts occasionally doing double duty. Though the prompts themselves vary, my purpose in giving them is designed to subtly teach intellectual behaviors practiced by successful learners. The prompts fall into these habits of mind:

◆ Reflection and goal setting around course objectives, with an emphasis on inquiry. (Chapter 4)
◆ Helping students locate their own, original thinking (rather than parroted thinking) around a concept or subject area. (Chapter 5)
◆ Teaching aspects of the curriculum through writing exercises. (Chapter 6)
◆ Generating ideas for assigned student writing. (This is where Joey's lesson sticks with me. Even in science it is unfair to thrust students into developing formal papers without a time and place for rumination. Teachers can model what real authors do to gather their thoughts through prompting.) (Chapter 7)

Because the pages in the notebooks for collected writings are numbered, it is not necessary to divide the notebook into categories as I was tempted to do in early attempts at writer's notebooks. Having the notebook organized in advance was a deterrent to getting students writing because I was always struggling with "How do I organize this? Where will I tell them to store this idea?" Thoughts are not linear. Later we can employ an organizing tool and do not need to preplan every move of our students in advance. The page numbers will be our tool. Leaving space for an index resolves the problem of organizing by subject matter or question types. (Some leave blank pages in the front of a notebook for building a Table of Contents in the same fashion—categorizing after writing.) Students can reread passages and categorize them later, either on their own or at the teacher's direction. For example, a teacher might ask students to create an index item called "Causes of the Civil War" and have students collect all page numbers for entries which fall under this category. Categorizing information is also a task that further enhances learning. Letting students do this independently mimics yet another intellectual behavior that mirrors the categorization exhibited by divisions of genus and species in science, functions of words in English, time periods in history and geology, and so forth.

As you will see in the chapter on assessment (Chapter 8), students can be required to mine their Daybooks for evidence of learning, marking passages where they feel they demonstrate an understanding of a concept on their own and then sharing that entry with you. Asking that these entries be marked for your observation also relieves teachers of the need to collect and respond to every piece of writing. One teacher I know has developed a routine "Daybook Quiz" where students are given questions they must answer by finding their response in the notebook. This reinforces the idea that student writing is an important tool for capturing learning. Locating places where they exhibit an understanding lets them practice the intellectual tasks of evaluating and assessing. Additionally, if students are sharing verbally in the classroom on a regular basis, circulating and listening in on the reading should provide teachers with an ongoing formative assessment of student understanding.

Summing Up

How a teacher phrases a prompt has a great effect on student success in constructing a response. Nevertheless, most teachers should remember that daily writing is about collecting thinking in the student's own voice first and foremost. Writing which is graded for correctness should not interfere with the need to fluently create thought in text. Graded writing should come much later. Give thought to the nature of the questions. They will drive how the student responds.

For the Daybook, Incorporate the Following:

◆ Consider levels of questions to prompt the level of thought required. Questioning corresponds to Bloom's taxonomy of thinking.
◆ Let students know how responses will be used. Will they share these? Is it private thinking? Are you collecting for discussion or a paper?

◆ Provide prompts which allow for student choice. Choice ensures that every student will complete the writing with some degree of success.

◆ Reward students for what they do well. Students will return to a pleasant task again and again.

◆ Prompt students so they can practice intellectual behaviors like reflecting, inventing, thinking independently, and collecting for later products.

◆ Bring students in on categorizing, evaluating, and assessing their own learning with the Daybook.

The next four chapters will review the different prompting types: reflecting, inventing, thinking independently, and collecting. We begin with the intellectual behaviors of reflecting, goal setting, and questioning.

4

Where Have We Been?
Where Are We Going?

Prompting Reflection and Goal Setting
With an Emphasis on Inquiry

"By three ways may we learn wisdom: First, by reflection, which
is noblest. Second, by imitation, which is easiest; and third by
experience, which is the bitterest."

—Confucius

"We do not learn from experience. We learn from reflecting on
experience."

—John Dewey

What to Expect

When we reflect on experience we make meaning from it. But looking at
what we have done also helps us set goals for the future and ask questions about those experiences that spur us on to new goals. This chapter
is about helping students with their thinking around school experience.
These prompts help students tie learning to their lives in the outside world.

Chapter Topics

  ◆ Understanding reflection as a process that supports learning.
  ◆ Determining where and when to interrupt instruction for
    reflection and goal setting.
  ◆ Activating reflection through questions.
  ◆ Tying reflection to specific assignments.

Reflection and Response in Any Content

How do we know when we have learned something? In recent years, schooling has been narrowed to rote response, Level 1 question (page 53) and answer. Unfortunately, learning this way does not stick. Irrelevant material—at least material deemed irrelevant by a student—is quickly jettisoned after testing, defeating our goals. The real goal of education is to change behaviors or paradigms of thought. Learning has taken root when the experience has altered our thoughts or behaviors, and we can apply that learning to new situations. Just like the adage "Give a man a fish and he eats for a day. Teach a man to fish and he eats for a lifetime," we need to provide students with repeatable processes—fishing—that are adaptable and applicable in future situations. The first and last step in the learning process should provide an opportunity to review and codify learning through reflection. Writing is a powerful tool for reflection. Its linear nature forces students to process and make sense of experiences.

In a study by Harvard Business School and the University of North Carolina (Di Stefano 2014, p. 3), researchers discovered that post-lesson reflection has a positive effect on learning. In the study, it did not matter whether the reflection was shared or not; the learning gains were still realized. Participants were instructed to write out specifically what they had done to complete a task. The study supports the idea that this kind of writing does not need to be scored to have an effect; however, collecting the writing and reading it is a beneficial window for instructors into each student's individual gains or misconceptions.

A particularly articulate student expressed her satisfaction with writing out her thoughts this way:

> I enjoyed writing the reading logs because I could really see my
> thought process at work. Instead of just meandering my way

through a book, I was purposefully sitting down and writing out what I thought. It slowed me down, allowing me to notice new details of a book and connect things in different ways. Also, when we shared our logs with each other, I got to hear other people's impressions about the book. It focused my thoughts, so that if I needed to clarify something that had happened, I could. If I had a question, I could ask it (albeit on paper that wasn't going to answer me) but it would then be in my head for me to think about.

(senior, female, 2012)

Note how the reflective logs provide an opportunity for the student to set her own purpose for learning. The requirement of stopping and writing to capture thought offered the chance to both review and then question the reading. The questioning then drives the purpose for the next reading session, sometimes far beyond what a teacher might think is important or relevant.

Reflection must be practiced and, for some students, the metacognition required to answer reflective questions must be directly taught. Unlike the student quoted above about the response logs, a very self-reflective and observant young woman, other students need repeated practice in examining their own learning—especially if they have never had an opportunity to review experience. When I was growing up, my family gathered at the dinner table each evening and, I realize now, a part of our conversation included a review of the day—a reflection, if you will. We were constantly sharing and evaluating experience through talk. In households where this habit of mind is not supported, the schools must provide the habit. In some classes, I provide lots of scaffolding questions to get these students started down the road to reflecting on and evaluating experience. (See Appendix B for Initial Self-Assessment on reading and the Change Paper.)

Though some students will need practice in noticing their own thinking, the results of reflection can be personally gratifying to students who see intelligence as fixed. Regularly revisiting changes in understanding builds self-confidence in the ability to realize change. The likelihood that the learning experience can be repeated in the future in differing situations is increased.

In addition to providing students with stems or prompting questions, some may find it helpful to change the medium before writing. This cartoon graphic in Figure 4.1 may invite some students into revisiting their experiences before writing about them.

Some students may need support in building their reflective powers. Try shifting the media to drawing to help students get at their thoughts.

Figure 4.1 Student sample: My Writing Process.

An additional bonus of providing reflection time that makes learning visible to students is an increased sense of self-efficacy. As Carol Dweck has revealed (*Mindset*, 2006) students can learn that intelligence is not fixed and we can influence a student's belief in him or herself as a capable learner. An ongoing personal record of a student's learning over time will reveal to most students that they do have some control over their own learning and that effort and persistence can result in real change.

Reflection and Goal Setting

It is tempting to dive right into material at the beginning of every course since time is always nipping at our heels. But reflection and goal setting are two activities that will do the most to help students transform their lives through your teaching. This is a case where slowing down in the initial phases of a course or unit will help both you and the students speed up afterward.

Early prompts in the Daybook can help students identify themselves as learners in your subject area. This kind of self-exploration helps students locate skills they may already have to succeed but are either unaware of or have not reflected on. This writing is exploratory and need not be collected, though as Peter Elbow suggests, for those students who are well trained to avoid work unless it is collected, do so (Elbow "Grading"). Once work is collected, teachers can either award points or simply read over it for insights into student understanding. As students become accustomed to regular, exploratory writing, they come to value the activity.

Reflective writing offers the opportunity to review learning, take it in, and own it. A natural follow up to looking backward is to look forward in the form of goal setting. In goal setting, students set a very personal purpose for learning in the classroom. Though the two activities seem at opposite ends of the spectrum, they work together simultaneously. You must first look back at where you have been and how you got there before you can look forward to see where you are headed, applying those skills initially used for previous successes. Writing helps students look both backward and forward. This chapter will demonstrate prompts that can aid students in discovering what they know and what they want or need to know next.

Teacher Tip

Students who have had little opportunity to reflect in other situations will need more help. Provide sentence stems or prompting questions. Appendix B has a collection of prompts to help students look both backward and forward in their learning.

Start the Year by Looking Backward

At the beginning of a course or unit, teachers can help students enter the topic with prompts that ask them to define or set the purpose of the daily meetings. Students in my English class spend the first day reflecting on who they are as readers. We spend time going backward to see how they ended up in senior English. I model responses to the prompts with my own experience—as I get to know them, they get to know me and how my experiences led to my role as their English teacher. We spend our first meeting writing and sharing as is described in earlier chapters. Though the prompt is similar to topics used in a Daybook, the students do not yet have that tool and will write on available paper. They will use the writing created that first day, sometimes just abbreviated notes or lists, to complete an informal essay titled "Myself as a Reader." We spend lots of time figuring out the trajectory of that story. They also get to know my own peculiar quirks as a reader. Later we will explore their writing selves.

First, they are asked to remember who they were before they were readers. Can they remember if anyone read to them? What were their favorite books? What was a book that they loved to hear, maybe over and over? Students write and then share and steal forgotten memories from their tablemates as they begin to discover the history of their reading. Peers often fill in the blanks of book titles and authors far better than I who was exposed to a different library of children's books.

We then move on to what they can remember reading from the time when they first learned to read. What book(s) do you remember reading independently? Tell the story of your entry into the world of reading. After that we move on to "Chapter Books," "Books I Was Proud to Have Read," and, finally, "My Last Favorite Book" and "A Book That Changed My Life" so that the joy and power of reading to learn is underscored. The entire period is spent reviewing the history of their reading life—which is relatively brief as a life goes since most of these students have only been readers for about nine years. The mood in the classroom is celebratory as all review how far they have come.

Once established as readers, the group then compiles a list of the "Criteria for a Good Book." In a course on analyzing literature, I want to capitalize on their existent expertise as critics on the very first day. The criteria establish a student-created evaluative tool they can use for any of the reading completed in the course. Next, students are directed to choose one of the common texts they have read and apply their tool to an analysis of the text as a "good" book. An objective for the course, and all the writing, is to build confidence in students as alert readers who can make evaluative claims without relying on "expert" critics, who generally have PhDs earned after years of professionally analyzing text.

In terms of the prompting, note how it has moved rather seamlessly from the reflective (who have you been as a reader?) to the goal setting (how will you or can you evaluate text?). Reviewing experience uncovers the skills that the students already possess and are ready to apply in a new situation. This is how the reflection leads naturally into the setting of goals.

As was stated in Chapter 2, once we start using the Daybook, the first homework prompt after beginning daily writing is to write a page in response to the questions *Why study literature? What do you consider litera-ture? Is it worthwhile reading?* Students are directed to fill an entire page. The full-page requirement is an effort to get students to push past their first reflexive answer and to think about the purpose or lack of purpose to the course itself. Even if a student does not agree that the course is worthwhile, he or she will have, at the very least, considered why the course is even offered and will hear the opinions and reasons provided by an important social group, peers. Passive students comply with assignments without understanding either their purpose or usefulness to their lives. We owe it to them to provide the time and space to think about what they will be doing for the next year or semester.

This reflection is followed the next day with a frank discussion in which students are permitted to answer the question in any way they see fit. The debate is not frivolous. This is an argument that is current in education circles. The emphasis on non-fiction and argument writing has prompted many universities and secondary schools to defend a liberal arts program.

Former biology teacher Bob Tierney framed the overriding objective of science to his students as a search for the truth. His early prompting for thinking was to ask students, *How do you know something is true?* or *When have you encountered something you believed to be true that changed the way you thought? Have you ever changed your mind about something you once thought was true? Why did you?* From these early writings both a purpose for the course and an entry into scientific thought is introduced. In a history class, we might begin by asking students, *What is your history on this planet? How do you know your entire history? Does the story of your life change depending on who is telling it (mom, dad, sister, brother)?* These questions can lead to the big idea of "Who gets to write the history of the world?" Now we are thinking as historians and scientists rather than passive receivers of a tale told through someone else's lens.

Entering a unit with large objectives and essential questions clearly in mind helps in formulating prompts. Teachers can link essential questions to a student's personal experience. A good stem for a prompt might be "Write about a time when . . ." and then invite the student to think about their own experiences with the underlying concept. Notice the open language of "about a time when" which provides an opening for a student to choose any event in their lives which fits the criteria of the rest of the prompt, whether it is school related or not. There is an implied choice in the phrasing. This opening is an opportunity for every student to succeed at the task. It also brings their non-school lives into the classroom and course of study, providing a natural connection to their current selves. When shared immediately with peers, the gap between the personal life and school begins to close.

In an English class, the underlying themes of any text can become the prompt initiating student thought around the concepts they will soon encounter in the action or words of a drama, narrative, or poem. For example, if you know *courage* will be a central theme, start student writing with the prompt: "Describe an act of courage you have witnessed. What happened? Why do you consider it courageous?" In writing, students discuss the event and then develop their own definition of courage prior to reading. If the writing is shared, students will hear multiple definitions of courage and potentially realize that this concept has a variety of interpretations. The subsequent reading becomes an automatic comparison to the student's perhaps newly adjusted definition of courage, shaped and considered in respect to the differing views of the classroom. The prompt itself begins the student's journey into considering why and how courage reveals itself in his or her own life.

In science, a central process is the scientific method. Before introducing the steps, ask students to *Write about a time when you figured something out. What did you do? How did you know you figured it out?* The focus of this prompt is on process and can lead to a rich discussion on problem solving, observation, collecting evidence, and other techniques of inquiry. Discussions are even richer when a student answer is not connected to schoolwork. Students can see the process of their minds at work in the wider world and bring that awareness into tackling what may seem to be daunting work.

> **✓ Teacher Tip**
>
> Watch for students who do not write. These are students who have had little practice reviewing their experiences and are our strugglers. Quiet encouragement with additional questioning helps. Knowing about the student's life and interests is particularly helpful in prompting memories. It is *most important* that these students are exposed to the reflections of their peers for examples of how the minds of others work. It takes time and patience to bring these students into reflective thought. Strugglers need more praise and encouragement and less negative consequence.

The key is to transform objectives into questions, and connect the question to personal experience. You will note that none of the questions results in a yes or no answer. Remember, questions structured this way may prompt a student to answer *no* and avoid the task. For instance, if you ask, *Can you remember a time when . . . ?* a student might think, *No, I can't*, and then will not participate in the thinking.

Sometimes teachers can create an experience for writing in the classroom. For instance, when introducing a unit on the eye, invite students to closely observe another student's eye, draw it, and then ask questions based on what they have seen. This sparks our natural curiosity. In this case, the prompt is an interesting artifact. In a math class provide a real-world problem and invite students into imagining a solution to the problem. *How would you go about figuring this out? What might you do first? Think of as many ways as possible.* Engaging student curiosity through writing creates students who are willing partners in inquiry. In a health class ask students to log their eating for a week and then bring the log to class for questioning and discussion around healthy eating. In a math class have students log the ways numbers show up in their daily lives for perhaps three or four days. Center a discussion or reflection on where and how math intersects with their everyday lives. Turn their daily interactions into a place for thoughtful reflection.

Early prompts in the Daybook can help students identify themselves as learners in your subject area. This kind of self-exploration helps students target skills they already have and can transfer but have previously been unaware of or have not reflected on. This writing is exploratory and, if read, should take into consideration only the ideas presented rather than the correctness of the structure of the writing. Correctness, at this point, is missing the point entirely. What we want to locate is student thought.

Tools for Reflection

Two easy tools for giving students time to reflect on their personal experience with new content are **response writing** and responding to **reflective questions**.

Response Writing

When students are faced with new content, encourage a response to the new knowledge. For example, assign a short reading. Then, rather than answer end-of-chapter questions that demand recall (or can often be answered without an engaged reading), ask students to pull what they feel are the two, three, or four (you choose) most important lines from the reading and then defend their choice through writing. *Why are these the most important lines?* This prompt alone more fully engages the student in the reading as they must be thinking and evaluating the material as they read. Students can share and argue their choices in class. The writing, the sharing, and the arguing are all methods that encourage wrestling with new material and connecting it to personal experience. We want to form intellectual habits that ask us to think critically as we read, questioning, arguing, and defending the ideas presented.

With longer readings, like a book, ask students to stop and write at points in the reading to record their thinking (Figure 4.2). This is the assignment the student refers to in the student writing at the beginning of this chapter on the helpful nature of the logs to her learning. Students were asked to divide their reading into thirds and then stop and write about 500 words on their thoughts about the reading. The linear nature of the writing helps students sort through the new knowledge and its effect on them. If students are new to response writing, you can provide them with a list of questions to spur thought.

These logs are shared on the due dates for completing the reading. The group discusses this portion of challenging reading together, both helping each other with tough passages and clarifying text meaning as they go. The shared readings also reveal many similar reactions to the characters and the plot, underscoring that these reactions might be geared toward the author's purpose. Questions such as, *So why does the author want us all to feel this way? What is the implication?* help students define an author's purpose. Responses can also be drawn from students on non-fiction reading (Figure 4.3). By requiring a response, teachers demonstrate that any text should be combined with a reader's experience and critical thought for full comprehension and the ability to apply learning to new situations.

Figure 4.2 Example of a response journal for literature.

How to Write a Response Journal

When assigned a response journal, use the following guidelines: divide your reading into three parts. If you are reading a three-act play, the division should be obvious—write a response at the end of each act.

Write your first response at the end of the first third, your second response at the end of the second third, etc. Do the writing **AS YOU READ**. Don't wait until finishing the work to complete the writings. The response journal is just that: a record of how you are responding emotionally and thoughtfully to the work and combining it with your experiences.

Your response should be one page in length or approximately 500 words. Please **word-process** your response, unless you have made other arrangements with me. Make a header for your pages that includes an MLA style citation for the book you are responding to.

What should you write about? If you get stuck for topics you may use the following questions as a guide. Do not, however, feel yourself limited or directed by these questions.

1. What are your feelings after finishing the section?
2. Does the story make you laugh, cry, smile, cheer, explode? Where and why?
3. How is this book like or not like your own life?
4. What are the best parts? What are the worst?
5. What seems most believable? What is incredible?
6. What is the author saying about life and living through this book?
7. Do you think the title fits the book/play/poem? Why or why not?
8. Did you like the ending? Why or why not?
9. What is the most important word, sentence, or passage? The most important event, character, feeling, or decision? Why?
10. In what ways are you like any of the characters?
11. What makes you wonder in this book/play/poem?
12. What came as a surprise in the book?

Figure 4.2 (Continued)

13. Has this book helped you in any way? Explain.
14. How do you picture the author of this book/play/poem? Why do you picture him/her this way?
15. What questions would you like answered after reading this book/play/poem?

Figure 4.3 Example of a response journal for non-fiction reading.

How to Log Your Reading in Non-Fiction

When assigned a response journal, use the following guidelines:
Divide your reading into three parts. You will log your thinking after reading each third. There should be three entries per book.
Write your first response at the end of the first third, your second response at the end of the second third, etc.
Do the writing **AS YOU READ**. Don't wait until finishing the work to complete the writings. The response journal is just that: a record of how you are responding emotionally and thoughtfully to the work and combining it with your experiences.
Your response should be approximately 500 words. Please **word-process** your response, unless you have made other arrangements with me.
Make a header for your pages that includes the title, author, publisher, publication date, and YOUR NAME.
What should you write about? Whatever thinking that has rippled through your mind as you read. Remember this is NOT a SUMMARY. It is a record of your thoughts.
If you get stuck for ideas, here are some prompting questions to choose from.

1. Why is this topic important? Why should others read this book?
2. How is the topic of this book similar to others you have read? How is it different?
3. Make a list of what new items you have learned by reading this.
4. What confirms your understanding?

5. What would you argue against as observed in your experience?
6. What ideas do you find compelling? How do they make you do further thinking?
7. What is the author's purpose of your book? Explain how you know.
8. Explain what you feel while reading this book. Why do you feel this?
9. What pictures, illustrations, diagrams, or photographs are helpful? Explain how/why they help.
10. Explain why a friend should/should not read this book.
11. What part of the book was the most interesting? Why did this stick out?
12. Would you like to read more books about this topic? Explain why or why not.
13. Does the author explain new concepts to you? Give an example. What are you still unsure of?
14. What questions would you ask the author if he/she came to your school?
15. If you were the author explain what you would do *differently*.
16. Explain why you enjoyed or did not enjoy this book. Be specific.
17. Compare and contrast events or concepts from the selection.
18. How is the information that you have read similar or different from other texts (or what you already know) about the subject?

Reflective Questions for Looking at Process

When teaching a process—like experiments in science, algorithms in math, creating media, developing a proposal—prompt students with reflective questions to review their intellectual work. Ask them to examine:

◆ Why did you choose this problem?
◆ Which questions were easy to solve? Why?
◆ Which are hard to solve? Why?
◆ When solving x, what should you do first? Second? (And so forth.) Finally?
◆ In conducting your experiment, what should you do first, second, etc.?

- ◆ Why do you consider your experiment a success or failure?
- ◆ What else do you think I should know about this project?
- ◆ Explain how to conduct this experiment if you were helping a third grader. (Switching audiences is a great test of student knowledge.)
- ◆ What is the hardest part of _____?
- ◆ What is the easiest part of _____?
- ◆ What would you do differently next time?

Students can share these reflections with their peers, resolve sticking points, or rework problems and experiments. The writing, however, will help students absorb their own idiosyncratic process and make thinking visible.

As is true with both writings—reflective and responsive—there is no real "wrong" answer to the writing since it is merely the collection of student thought in its rawest form. However, teachers find these writings informative in terms of how students are understanding material. Collecting and reading these writings, though not scoring them on formal conventions, is an ideal formative assessment since it is a window into a student's mind. They do not need to be collected if you are listening in on conversations where the writing is shared or asking students to briefly write about what was gained in the sharing or reviewing on an exit ticket.

> **Teacher Tip**
>
> Exit tickets are a common write-to-learn reflective activity. Provide about five minutes at the end of class for students to summarize their learning for the day. The "tickets" are handed to the teacher on the way out the door to secure an exit. These are quick formative assessments for learning and require every student to produce a reflective summary of the day.

Reflective Question Framework for Adaptation

The general premise of reflection is to frame questions in three subcategories. Asking our students questions that fit into the categories fosters the intellectual habit of reviewing work, evaluating its usefulness, and setting the goal for the next step:

What happened? Inspire students to report what they did or did not do. No interpretation of the events is necessary.

So what? This is an opportunity to consider what was learned and what difference, if any, the event made. Feelings, ideas, and some analysis are all a part of considering the effect of the event on the student.

Now what? Here students can synthesize the experience of the event plus project into the future how they might see themselves applying the new learning in a different situation.

The question stems below can help students move from reflection to inquiry or supposing, another intellectual tool which is rarely cultivated in curriculum-driven classrooms.

Adapt these stems to your content area and let all students write freely.

◆ What do you need to do next?
◆ Based on what you know, what can you predict about . . . ?
◆ Suppose . . . . What then?
◆ How about . . . ?
◆ What if . . . ?
◆ When is another time you need to . . . ?
◆ What is another way to . . . ?
◆ How is . . . different from (or like) . . . ?
◆ How would you feel if . . . ?
◆ What do you think causes . . . ?

Here are questions I use to direct students through reflection after they have developed a processed paper from inception to final draft. Each time we have an extended writing assignment, students collect their drafts as evidence of their writing journey and write a preface based on the questions. I rewrite my questions each time to reflect what went on in the classroom as the piece developed. Notice question number four references specific mini-lessons we did around identified skills which were directly taught and practiced in the Daybook.

1. How did you get your idea?
2. Did your idea change as it went along? How?
3. How did your peer group help or hinder you through your weekly meetings?
4. How did you use/not use the mini-lessons on writing good beginnings, showing vs. telling, CRISPing your writing?
5. If you had more time, what would you do?
6. What else would you like me to know?

Reading student responses prior to examining their work reveals whether students are internalizing the skill lessons taught as the paper progresses. A sample student response appears in Figure 4.4. Students are also very forthcoming in their responses. The final question, "What else do you want

Figure 4.4 Sample student reflection on writing. (A blank questionnaire is available in Appendix B.)

Preface to the Writing

1. **Where did you get your idea? Did it change as you went along?**
    I got my idea from personal experience. I was suicidal at one point, but now I see why killing myself wouldn't solve anything. I wanted to put what I learned in the story as well as express my feelings. I didn't give the character a name at first, but in my continuation of my story in my daybook, I gave her a name. Originally I wanted the reader to be the character or witness the pain, feelings, and thoughts before associating her w/ a name or as a separate person.

2. **What audience did you intend for this piece? How successful do you think you were at reaching the audience? Why?**
    I intended the readers to be teenagers, specifically depressed and suicidal teenagers, but also those who have not experienced the depression so they can see and experience the effects. I think I am fairly successful at reaching the audience because the reader can follow her thoughts and connect.

3. **Explain how the mini-lessons did/did not impact your piece.**
    I think I crisped more especially after the lesson. It helped take away extraneous words & focused the writing more.

4. **Describe the peer review experience and its usefulness/detriment to writing.**
    The peer review helped me to gain more courage and motivation to write/in my writing. They encouraged me.

5. **If you had more time, what would you do?**
    I would add to my piece to make it more complete because I have more drafts to the story.

6. **Is there anything else you think I should know about this piece?**
    I put a lot of myself in this story. It is important to know that it is an anti-suicide story, but I meant for it to connect readers to the story to know and realize they are not alone.

    —Female, senior

me to know?" has always resulted in answers which have the ring of truth. Students also like this question because it opens the door to explaining themselves and what might have helped or hindered completion of a piece of work. Frequently, students answer, "There is nothing else you need to know."

Other Reflective Prompting

Though the basis for reflective prompting is all the same (*What happened? What did it mean? What can you do with this information?*), there are a few ways to get at student thinking around our curriculum. Here is a collection of writing activities that can be adapted to content area courses. Besides these, don't forget the powerful prompts: *What do you notice? What questions do you have? What do you already know?*

Activity #1: Provide a Stimulus

Prior to a starting a unit, develop readiness by either inspiring curiosity or determining the level of background knowledge. Try starting with an old photograph, a map, a news article, or some artwork in history; several pieces of art or music prior to working with the media or a thematic unit in the arts; introduce an self-assessment of a student's current state of health before a physical fitness activity; engineer a close observation for a biology or environmental science unit. Follow the introduction of these objects with the simple prompts, *Write about what you notice. What questions do you have?*

Activity #2: Post-Reading Writing

Assign a short reading for either in-class or for homework. Ask students to evaluate what they have read by asking them to: *List the most important ideas from this reading with number one being the most important. Give your reasons for each item on the list.*

Or: *Pull the most important line (or two/three lines) from the work. Why is it important?*

These writings should be shared in small groups so that all students have time to hear each other, process the material, and then debate the most important ideas. The group consensus can be shared with the larger group, thus rehashing the ideas once again. All students get the opportunity to hear the central ideas again, pick up on information or thoughts they might have missed initially, and reconsider major concepts.

Finally, after hearing all of the discussion, students should write again: *What is the most important idea you will be taking away from this discussion? How does that idea fit in with our course of study?* This writing can be turned in as a formative assessment, to see student understanding or saved in the Daybook for review later. In addition to learning content, students are learning a framework for learning from independent reading and note making. This is the critical thinking Daniel Willingham indicates must go on within the context of the content.

Activity #3: Gratitude Journaling

So much of life—and especially schooling—operates from a deficit model. We are always asking, *What's missing? What is missing in a student's understanding? What personal possessions do I wish I had? Why aren't I: prettier, smarter, thinner, more popular?*

All of us can benefit from looking at our world and experiences from the abundance side of the coin. It makes our lives richer and more fulfilling. I encourage you to include some reflection at periodic times throughout the year that prompts students to reflect with gratitude.

For instance, *What has science added to your life in a positive way? What are you grateful to have learned about our shared history? Who in your family/neighborhood/circle of friends is a great resource for what we are learning? Why? What has changed you for the better because of what we are learning here today?*

Occasionally I take time to refocus students on what is going well in their lives. During the month of November, the American month for Thanksgiving, I challenge them to make a gratitude entry in their Daybooks each day of the month to reflect on something good from that day. To get them started on this challenge, we watch Louie Schwartzberg's beautiful film shown in his TED talk "Nature. Beauty. Gratitude."

For seniors at the end of their schooling, we refocus on increasing our happiness by letting someone know we are glad to have them in our lives. I use the lesson "A Simple and Effective Lesson on Gratitude" posted by Larry Ferlazzo at his "Website of the Day" (http://larryferlazzo.edublogs.org/2013/11/22/a-simple-effective-classroom-lesson-on-gratitude/).

Activity #4: Facts/Values Lists

Before beginning a new topic, have students create lists. What they already *know* should be listed on the left-hand side of the page. What they *believe, feel, or suspect* should go on the right-hand side of the page. Share, share, share to gather an introduction created by the whole class.

Students can return to these lists at the end of the unit to see how their thinking has changed. Ask them to write an entry on the changes they have seen. This is an excellent reflective writing that will cement the new growth.

Activity #5: First Thoughts
Students write or list their initial impressions about a topic they are about to study. Refer to these at the end to gauge new learning and understanding. Students can write about their growth or gaps in their knowledge at the end of a unit.

Activity #6: Position Papers
This paper is an initial writing in a course or a unit. In it the student does what has been suggested in both the *facts/values* lists and the *first thoughts* prompt. The Position Papers can be a first and last activity in the Daybook or writing turned in for review. In an initial Position Paper, the student writes out his or her position in regards to the topic under discussion. Encourage students to describe past experiences with the topic which may be positive or negative, and their current position or understanding of the subject. This can be especially helpful in uncovering negative experiences from past schooling that are a huge barrier to approaching the topic. This writing should be informal and should be read by the instructor as an introduction to the student and their current thinking, to glean what is known, not how it is expressed. When students sense that you are truly interested in their experiences, they will be forthcoming. Subjects that are continually defeating for some students—can benefit from the opportunity to air grievances. Teachers who fail to address students' emotions toward a subject will be swimming upstream throughout the year. These papers are extremely informative at the beginning of a course.

The initial position should be referred to at the end of the unit/course as a basis for writing the final Position Paper. Students should refer to their initial position to see how they have moved within the content and describe how they have changed. Not only will the teacher have a clear picture of what the student has or has not gained, the student writing will reveal the knowledge that this student now owns and the student will also *know what he knows*.

Activity #7: Change Papers
This is very like the ending Position Paper. To write a Change Paper, a course or a unit must begin with an initial survey of content knowledge and goal setting around course skills and content. I use an initial survey

and ending Change Paper with students who are not naturally reflective because the two tools prompt student metacognition. In a reading and writing class in the age of standardized testing, we are continually pretesting students on their skill level. In my English classes I have always shared the pretests, their scores, and an explanation of the skills tested so students can review and evaluate their own work. We then set goals for learning. The final post-testing and other artifacts of the course become the gauge for any changes. With the data and course products in front of them (generally collected in an in-class portfolio of some sort) the students use the prompting on the Change Paper assignment to reflect on their learning. Without this final reflection, students may not have any awareness of what they gained throughout our time together. Without a review of the work, separate assignments are simply disjointed busywork rather than building to a new skill level. Students need this time to make sense of the weeks of our demands for practice. A sample Change Paper assignment appears in Appendix B.

Activity #8: Portfolios

There is little that I have done that has meant more to students than the collecting and reflecting on two semesters of work. In a portfolio modeled on Sheridan Blau's *The Literature Workshop: Teaching Texts and Their Readers* (2003) my students collect everything they have produced in the course, sort it into self-selected categories, and then reflect on each of the categories and its usefulness—or lack of—to learning. Students must create and explain their own divisions of the work. The entire body of work is also ascribed a meaning—or the *meaning of the work as a whole*—to borrow the language of the Advanced Placement testing the students have grown familiar with—in a general introduction. Finally, students select from among their artifacts examples of their best work, samples which show the three goals for our course: fluency, flexibility, and control. They are permitted to revisit any of the assignments they choose for their selection to revise and upgrade into the best possible product.

Students both groan and celebrate over this activity. However, after amassing their work, many are astounded at what they have produced and celebrate the achievement of so much in such a short span of time. This end-of-course reflection is by far more meaningful than a semester exam since students must consider all they have done and see it as a "whole" learning experience. As a bonus, students have returned from college stating that the artifact of their writing portfolio was used to gain entrance into writing-intensive or honors courses.

Back in the Real World

A portfolio can bring together all the assigned work from a long course. Arranging and collecting the work can let students see their accomplishments. Here is a typical response to collecting work:

> Flipping through my portfolio I feel amazed. It is much longer than I had originally anticipated. It is only now, seeing everything in one place that I realize how much work I have done this semester . . . . I was afraid that when I saw all of my work together I would be disappointed or embarrassed, but the opposite is true. I am proud of what I have accomplished this year. My reading logs and work with poetry show vast improvement in analysis over the year. In general, I think that my writing has also matured and improved and I am certainly faster. I have learned to be more creative and less dependent upon structured guidelines and norms. I feel confident that I demonstrate all of the skills necessary for college, the most important being the ability to learn and improve. In this course we have worked to understand ourselves and our thought processes with, in my opinion, a great degree of success. My portfolio is representative of myself as a reader, writer, and thinker, and viewing the final product, I am glad to be represented by it.
>
> (Cassie, senior)

 Teacher Tip

Opportunities for additional reflection and goal setting all appear in Appendix B. Additional opportunities for reviewing course work through the Portfolio and Change Paper, reflections on class Seminars (as well as how to run these), and questionnaires for students are all included.

Summing Up

Our students need time to absorb the lessons they are exposed to throughout a school year jammed with curriculum requirements. Writing reflectively is the tool that helps them see what they learned and that naturally leads them to ask questions and set goals for their next set of experiences. Use the Daybook to collect their thoughts about what they have learned.

For the Daybook, Incorporate the Following:

◆ Begin a unit or course of study with questions that help students locate the concepts and skills from previous experiences. They can apply the knowledge and skills to the experiences to come.
◆ Stop routinely to let students catch their breath around your teaching, especially after learning a new process. Writing provides time to review in their own language.
◆ Consider papers or portfolios that ask students to look at gains they have made over time—have them write about that.
◆ Be aware that reflective writing can let you see how each student is making sense of lessons. It is the ideal tool to differentiate for every student.

The next chapter explains prompting that drives students toward their own original thinking.

5

Wait. What? You Want My Opinion?

Helping Students Locate Their Own Thinking

"You write to discover what you want to say. You rewrite to discover
what you have said and then rewrite to make it clear to other people."
—Donald Murray

What to Expect

This chapter helps teachers incorporate prompts that feature student thinking, rather than "borrowed thinking." Rather than parroting others, these
prompts ask students to look to themselves as a source. We have long known
that our students need to confront new situations with critical thought. But
how do you encourage and practice the skill of critical thinking? Helping
students find their own original thoughts is the focus of this chapter.

Chapter Topics

- ◆ Highlighting and building on skills students already possess.
- ◆ Using regular expressive writing to prompt students into
  locating their own ideas.
- ◆ Engaging with open-ended activities that reward intellectual
  work rather than right answers.

Bringing Student Thinking Into the Classroom

As a senior in high school, I remember listening to classmates enthusiastically present an argument on some topic in government or English class and thinking, *I don't think I have any opinions about anything.* In my defense, I don't recall being *asked* for a viewpoint in most of my classes, outside of very rare class discussions and a few small group projects. We were largely empty vessels waiting to be filled.

Our students, when provided little to no opportunity to explore their thinking, must also feel they have little to contribute. But they are thinking all the time, as I was, using critical thinking tools that can be exposed and capitalized on in any content. The trick is to make their thinking, and the steps they take, visible to themselves.

Except for those with profound disabilities, there is not a student who walks through the classroom door incapable of employing the tools of critical thinking. All of us do this kind of thinking all the time. Routinely we make judgments based on experience and arrive at hypotheses that must be tested. This kind of everyday critical thought might take the form of: *Can I trust a friend to keep a secret? What evidence do I have of this person's trustworthiness and loyalty?* Or: *What will I wear today?* This daily decision might be based on any number of factors such as the current weather, acceptable fashion among valued peers, how much attention to draw to the self, or the activities anticipated for the day. Our students think critically all the time. Scaffolded assignments (opening windows and doors) reveal their thinking processes while also allowing students to write their way to clarity. Recognizing the tools through metacognition—thinking about thinking—means these everyday skills can be mindfully employed in new situations.

Encountering Thought With Expressive Writing

Expressive writing is especially apt for these explorations. Expressive writing (page 48) is unique and important to any writer because it is effectively a writer talking to him or herself about what the writer/reader (for they are one in the same) is thinking about. The very act of writing provides a trail of visible thought and that thinking can press the writer on to the next thought. One written thought leads to another. The writer literally converses with him or herself, playing out ideas or possibilities for later abandonment or refinement. We can teach students to follow their own logical thinking.

In his book *Writing at the Threshold*, Benton College professor Larry Weinstein encourages practice runs of expressive writing with his students so they can discover their own truths, and then write more coherent, and ultimately more interesting, papers. He provides what he calls *think tanks*. These are opportunities to capture the inner voice on paper and follow the logic. As students practice these writings, Weinstein would play what he calls *tuneless background music*. The music is his voice, coaching students into writing for thinking rather than writing with an outside, more demanding audience.

His tuneless background music is the script below repeated several times as students write. He encourages students to tune him out and simply write when they no longer need the coaching.

> Be sure that you're writing for yourself now, not for an audience. This is you speaking to you, thinking on paper.
>
> As a hunch—a possible answer to your question—occurs to you, put it down, play it out . . . then, test it.
>
> Keep it honest. Don't stick to some hunch that does not truly survive your testing. Try out *other* possible answers.
>
> Bring *all* your resources to bear: firsthand experience, secondhand experience, reasoning, intuition, etc.
>
> *Leave room for uncertainty.*
>
> Think about what gaps in your knowledge you may need to fill to be able to answer your question with more certainty—and about how you might fill those gaps.
>
> (Weinstein 2001)

It is no mistake that the open questions on Advanced Placement tests, which measure a student's ability to achieve college-level work, ask that our students think for themselves and apply the fundamentals of any subject area to new situations. This is the essence of understanding and is also an expectation in college-level work.

However, the critical thinking demanded for the AP exams is just as important to technology and the trades. Every level of work requires some degree of hypothesizing, testing, and problem solving. Mastery of a trade or academic work occurs when the processes of problem solving combine with years of experience and the two become a natural, shorthand way of arriving at solutions. It is this practice in thinking, and recognizing the tools brought to bear in new situations, that need to be included in every discipline.

To develop thinking we invite students into academic conversation and reward their attempts to puzzle out a supposition. Daybook writing can help students locate their own individual thoughts and see their reasoning capability.

Build Student Confidence in Original Thought

In this small section are a few activities that will help students locate their own unique ideas.

Activity #1: Write to a Penny

This exercise is adapted from Robert Pirsig's assignment to his college students. Pirsig, a professor of composition and the author of *Zen and the Art of Motorcycle Maintenance* (1974), was frustrated with his students' inability to think for themselves, choosing instead to mimic ideas gathered from other thinkers in their essays. His assignment asked students to write for an hour with a penny as their prompt. He urged the student writers to follow their thinking as they wrote continuously for the entire hour.

My directions to my students are the same, but we don't have an hour. I explain they should follow their own thinking and see where it leads. They start with the penny as a prompt for thinking, and see where that goes. They are only given seven minutes to write; however, they must write for the entire time, just following one thought after another.

At the end of the seven minutes, I ask them to reread what they wrote and to underline or circle the most interesting line. Then they move that line to a new page and follow it and their thinking again for another seven minutes.

Sharing is optional with this exercise, but the lesson is this: given no other influence, what do *you* think? When students are asked to audit their Daybook (see Chapter 8) and identify an Original Thought, many refer to this exercise as a time when they surprised themselves with an opinion of their own, unassigned by a classroom teacher.

Activity #2: Pull a Line

In the "Write to a Penny" exercise, students are directed to reread their writing and find a line that intrigues them. The line is then transferred to another blank page and becomes the prompt for a new writing. This activity helps students see that they have ideas worth pursuing. The blank page encourages students to explore this one idea devoid of the previous writing and potentially head off in a new and fresh direction. Use this technique at any time in the Daybook writings when the goal is to help students go further into and around a topic. Often students develop more questions around the topic that are unique to their own interests and needs.

Or, share a reading with the entire class—a poem, short article, or related children's book. Tell them in advance to pull a line to write to or to respond to the entire piece in writing. After reading aloud, provide quiet time for writing. Then share and discuss as usual.

 Teacher Tip

Children's books are ideal for introducing and teaching content at any age. A quick search online for "children's books to teach [science, art, history, literary elements]" results in many titles and sample lessons for engaging secondary students.

Activity #3: Find a Slice of Life

This Daybook exercise has several objectives. Like the "Write to a Penny" exercise above, my chief objective in the literature course is helping students find and support their own opinions and reactions to the readings, videos, and discussions. I want them creating their own knowledge by examining their thinking and developing a unique voice. The "Slice of Life" activity helps them see that they have experiences and responses to add to the general discussion.

Students first read several essays that fall into the slice-of-life category. These are usually first-person commentary by leading columnists. They follow the general pattern of relating an experience and then observing their thinking around the event and drawing a conclusion from the experience. As I tell my students, these are often columns that can be found at the back of a favorite periodical (if anyone still receives these!) or are the stuff of blogs.

Back in the Real World

A sample slice of life from my blog.
Playing the Game of Life . . .
literally.
On the long drive back from the beach this month, I played *Life* on the cellphone app my daughter handed to me.
"It's fun. Try it."

It had been a good twenty years since I played the face-to-face board game when the kids were young. Back then the term "face-to-face" didn't even delineate a choice. All games were played face-to-face, even the ubiquitous video games. (My marker for the digital world is 1982, the year my son was born, and we bought an Apple. The first one. With the blinking cursor and the green text.)

The premise of the game is simple: whoever retires with the most money wins.

Though the spinner was fun, even responding to some finesse with touch, and the street-level view of the moving pieces was engaging, I found myself more and more angered as I progressed through my "life."

Everything was measured in money.

Birth of a child: receive $5,000 in gifts from friends. ($5,000? Really? No joy? No fulfillment? Just $5,000 bucks? A lousy measure of what the birth of my children meant to my husband and me. It was a hollow reward.)

College earned the player a lot more money right after graduation. The game choice I made—to go into entertainment—didn't pay well at all, but I picked it because it sounded like fun.

In the real game of life, my college years never really resulted in a big pile of money, but they were exciting and fulfilling. Choosing liberal arts changed me, changed my view of the world, and opened my awareness to a thirst for knowledge that has never abated. I'm not sure what dollar value I would place on that.

The game went on like that, with the milestones of a rich and varied life reduced to a dollar figure. I could hardly stand it. It seemed a little too real, a little too much like our current lives.

Numbers rule our lives here in America. Rich people are somehow better than poor. Those with high SAT scores are more valuable than those without. Wall Street must hit the numbers. School districts, teachers, students . . . all driven by the numbers. But for every number, especially the ones my students "earn," there is a whole story left untold.

Our focus on money and measurement has created a spiritual and cultural wasteland. Playing "who makes the most, scores the highest" is an unsustainable vision. It is simplistic, simple-minded, and a poor substitute for the richness of human experience. In addition, there can only be one winner at that game. It feels as though the piling up of wins would topple over from the sheer pressure to get more, more, more.

But it is something a businessman understands completely. And the business pros are winning at shifting this game into education.

My invisible, virtual opponent won the game. She retired before me and continued to play the numbers. She had taken an option out on the number "9" and it paid off several times, earning her well over a million dollars as she basked in retirement while I continued to limp along with my two-year degree. (I went back to school.)

She was divorced (big payout) and ended the game with only one child—no grandchildren.

I imagine her as a bitter old woman in a toney retirement home sipping martinis, playing backgammon, and yelling at the TV.

As for me, I lived a long, happy life in my log cabin surrounded by a pile of messy, disorganized grandchildren.

Guess I lose.

We look at several models of slice-of-life writings in class so the students can see how the columnist or blogger plays off the recent event to make a general observation. Part of the activity involves identifying features of the commentaries, yet another exercise in analysis that is easily accessible to students. All you must prompt students with is the question *What do you notice?* The slice-of-life essays also introduce another organic organization of an essay that stands in contrast to the five-paragraph tome taught in most secondary classrooms.

Students choose an event from the twenty events list (completed at an earlier time, see page 105 in Chapter 6) and write for seven minutes. Again, students are often surprised by their own opinions on their everyday experiences. They can produce a rather coherent commentary of some length in a short amount of time. Another goal is to convince students that an on-demand essay, often seen in testing situations, can be written rather quickly if you know what you are writing about. College entrance and some workplace exams require a timed essay. Planning and writing under time constraint is a skill they can develop. Seeing that producing coherent written thought in a brief amount of time is possible builds confidence in their own fluency.

Activity #4: Mimic Montaigne's *Essai*

The original *essai*—a French word translated loosely to mean "an attempt"—was Montaigne's recording of an attempt at understanding. You can elicit this type of thinking journey by taking students through an exercise that will reveal their reasoning, questioning, reliance on evidence and experience, supposing, and then concluding.

Before presenting something to read, tell your students you are going to give them something to read and then ask them to record the answer to this question: *What will I give you to read?* After they tell you their guesses, ask students to explain what they based their guess on. Likely they will reference some experience they have had with you, which you can point out as a valid thought process.

Then reveal the title on a Smart Board or other projection device and ask students to record their answer to the question *Now what do you think we will be reading about?* This time have students add some reasoning behind their answer by answering *What do you base that on?* Again, discuss the reasoning, rather than the answer to the question, to point out the intellectual moves that students are already making (reasoning, relying on evidence and experience, supposing). Congratulate them for the effort required to reason their way through the reading.

Move the students through the reading together, stopping at some pre-selected points to ask students to record what they are now thinking about the reading. Students should write down their thoughts and the reasoning which developed the thoughts in a simple t-chart. Placing the thought adjacent to the evidence underscores the relationship between the two. The chart creates a record of their shifting ideas. Continue until the entire piece has been read and discussed.

Students now have the fodder for a seamless discussion of their thinking as they read. They can develop this thinking into a Montaigne-style essay by adding in some smooth transitions. For instance, the essay might begin: *When Mrs. Tedrow told us she was going to read to us, I thought it would probably be something about teaching since she is always talking about teaching and learning. But then when I saw the title "A Road Less Traveled," I thought she was going to give us some vacation tips. It is almost summer so maybe she wants us to think about going on a trip. The less traveled road would probably be one that goes into the jungle or someplace cool like that.* Note the student is drawing on experience to formulate a clear reading of the passage. This is clear, visible reasoning.

Besides recording intellectual moves, this exercise shows students how important it is to think as you read to fully engage with the text. In academic classes this would naturally move into a discussion of annotating text to connect thinking with reading. Show students how to interact with the text by recording what is occurring in their minds in the margins.

Activity #5: Provide a Stem
Try these as starters to inspire original thinking in your students:

> *Of everything I've seen online this week . . .*
> *I recently witnessed a scene which made me think of . . .* (similar to the "Slice of Life" assignment. The twenty actions list would be helpful to generate ideas for this.)
> *I wonder if . . .*

Thinking Challenges to Push Students Into New Territory
Sometimes we need to push our students to go beyond their comfort zone. Occasionally dare students to push past their usual patterns of thought. Challenge them with these ideas:

Activity #6: Keep Writing
until you stumble upon a question that poses a real difficulty to consider.

Activity #7: Write 100 Questions
Do this writing quickly and don't stop until you have written 100 questions. After writing, look for any patterns to the questions. *What do they seem to lead to? Is there a theme?* Write about what you've noticed.

Activity #8: Don't Stop Writing
until you surprise yourself with an unusual connection. Sometimes I point out to students what they consider BS is often much deeper thinking. They are knitting together what seems to be unrelated ideas, and yet they are finding the commonalities. This is important thinking.

Activity #9: Play the Question and Answer Game
Have students write a question, any question, on one side of a 3x5 card. Students turn their questions face down and pass them to the right several times, without letting anyone else see their question. The receiver will write an answer, *any* answer, on the blank side of the card without looking at the question. Then pass the card again to the right. The receiver will read the question and the answer and then write an explanation for how the seemingly unrelated answer is correct for the question provided. Students can think

creatively around this puzzle. The answers are sometimes deeply insightful or full of humor.

Activity #10: Riddles and Puzzles

Start a class with a riddle or a puzzle. Rather than focusing on the correct answer, ask students to write about what they tested or thought about as they tried to resolve the puzzle. Emphasize the critical thinking tools they are bringing to bear on the problem, rather than the answer. Sharing in class means that all students benefit from hearing someone else's logic, which they can then borrow and use in new situations.

Activity #11: The Brain Dump

This is a *clear the decks* sort of writing. The directions are easy. Invite students to simply dump the contents of their mind onto the page. As a routine assignment, this can help students focus in the classroom. Whatever is causing worry, excitement, anticipation, or anxiety can be poured onto the page and held there. This clears the mind for the work of your classroom. Use this prompt after events of consequence so students can see what they are dealing with. If the event is important enough (a recent school shooting or the September 11 terrorist event come to mind), you can use the writing to get kids talking about coping with these universally important moments. A brain dump literally lets students see the contents of their mind.

Summing Up

We cannot expect our students to recognize and use critical thinking skills without clearing out a practice space. Every teacher has been repeatedly told that in a fast-moving world we do not know what our students will face in life choices or careers. We *do* know they will need to have the tools to make reasoned decisions. Use the content of your subject to get students thinking independently and practicing intellectual behaviors.

For the Daybook, Incorporate the Following:

◆ Provide open-ended opportunities for students to trace their thoughts.
◆ Incorporate short writings that ask students to act on a hunch and explain their reasoning. Focus on the reasoning.

- ◆ Routinely reward intellectual behavior while deemphasizing "right" answers.
- ◆ Tease out thinking through puzzles and riddles. Focus on the methods used to arrive at a conclusion.
- ◆ Invite students to regularly manipulate and extend the work going on in the classroom by thinking beyond the content.

The next chapter describes the promise of writing exercises which actually teach.

6

How Does Writing Support Course Objectives?

Teaching the Curriculum Through Writing

"Probably no subject is too hard if people take the trouble to think and write and read clearly."

—William Zinsser

What to Expect

This chapter shows ways to incorporate writing (and reading) into the classroom without sacrificing content. Some writing activities help students focus in on the essential questions of a course. Other activities assist students in accessing central concepts through the exercises.

Chapter Topics

- ◆ Shifting the work of the classroom from teacher talk to discovery and practice.
- ◆ Managing time to summarize and reflect on direct instruction.
- ◆ Using daily writing to transform and deepen learning.
- ◆ Using daily writing to understand concepts.

The Elephant in the Room Is Time

Probably the largest deterrent to using writing in the content areas is that teachers pressed to "cover" curriculum feel time is limited. It is important that content area teachers view writing in the classroom as an "instead of" and not just one more task to fulfill. Assigning writing should not be *added* to an already crowded plan. The writing should *replace* other, more standard practices. For instance, student writing followed by sharing and a large group discussion of pertinent points *replaces* a traditional teacher-led lecture with note taking, rather than being done *in addition to* traditional lecture.

Ideally, teachers will hew their curriculum down to a study of the most essential questions. A deep understanding of the major concepts will stick with students longer than rote memorization of isolated facts. Identifying these concepts is a worthwhile discussion for teachers who share instruction in the discipline.

A Paradigm Shift From Lecture to Constructing Learning

In my own teaching, I begin my planning by asking myself several questions: *How much of this do I have to do? How much of the thinking and discovery can I let my students do?* When I can devise a way for students to take over the discovery process, I plan for that instead of lecture. I found a chart in Mortimer Adler's manifesto on Socratic teaching, *The Paideia Proposal*, helpful to this decision-making process. In Figure 6.1, Adler divides hoped-for student outcomes into categories of teacher behavior which best serve the student. Try replacing your traditional teaching slowly until you get comfortable with how student activity can supplant other teacher-centered work.

This chart is helpful in determining which type of activity will serve the learning best. Many prompts fall into the category of both column two and three, spurring students to identify latent ideas.

We can help students access their own learning and model habits of scholarly behavior by providing time in class for students to read pertinent material and respond to it in writing, sharing, discussion, and note making. The difference between *note taking* and *note making* is this: note taking is a student record of *teacher* learning—the teacher constructed the notes from his or her own understanding of material. *Note making* is a student

Figure 6.1 When choosing activities for the classroom, Adler's chart focuses on student outcomes as a guide for planning.

COLUMN ONE	COLUMN TWO	COLUMN THREE
Student Outcome: ACQUISITION OF ORGANIZED KNOWLEDGE	Student Outcome: DEVELOPMENT OF INTELLECTUAL SKILLS, SKILLS OF LEARNING	Student Outcome: ENLARGED UNDERSTANDING OF IDEAS AND VALUES
by means of teacher facilitation through:	by means of teacher facilitation through:	by means of teacher facilitation through:
DIDACTIC INSTRUCTION LECTURES AND RESPONSES TEXTBOOKS AND OTHER AIDS	COACHING, EXERCISES, AND SUPERVISED PRACTICE	MAIEUTIC OR SOCRATIC QUESTIONING (bringing a person's latent ideas into clear consciousness) AND ACTIVE PARTICIPATION
in three areas of subject matter	in the operations of	in the
LANGUAGE, LITERATURE, AND THE FINE ARTS MATHEMATICS AND NATURAL SCIENCE HISTORY, GEOGRAPHY, AND SOCIAL STUDIES	READING, WRITING, SPEAKING, LISTENING CALCULATING, PROBLEM SOLVING, OBSERVING, MEASURING, ESTIMATING, EXERCISING CRITICAL JUDGEMENT	DISCUSSION OF BOOKS (NOT TEXTBOOKS) AND OTHER WORKS OF ART AND INVOLVEMENT IN ARTISTIC ACTIVITIES e.g. MUSIC, DRAMA, VISUAL ARTS

Adapted from MODES OF LEARNING AND TEACHING by Mortimer J. Adler
in *The Paideia Proposal*

record of *student* learning. Rather than dutifully copying notes from a Smart Board, students need the opportunity to process learning through their own expressive language. Whenever possible, replace lecture with reading, writing, sharing, and discussion.

Writing in the classroom becomes an opportunity to embrace the constructivist model of learning. The writing helps students construct, in their own accessible language, an individual understanding of the curricular concepts.

Back in the Real World

Studies have shown that our students are doing less and less reading outside of the school. This has had dramatic effects on literacy. The U.S. Department of Education has characterized student literacy levels as a "crisis." The National Assessment of Educational Progress (NAEP)—often referred to as the nation's report card—shows that fewer than a third of eighth graders read at the proficient level (Heller 2017). Over the years, student achievement in reading has been relatively flat while workplace demands for literate behaviors have risen. I don't know about you, but only my highest-achieving students tend to read outside of school. When we cannot rely on children to read independently, it is more important than ever to bring literacy practices into the classroom and provide both reading and writing time while we have the students with us.

Replace teacher talk with these activities where students create their own learning:

Activity #1: Stop and Write—Note Making

Sometimes, students simply need to have their background knowledge extended through direct instruction. In Adler's chart, this is the passing on of organized knowledge. When your lesson plans call for lecture, remember to build in opportunities to stop, write, share, and discuss, with the opportunity to revise notes.

As a rule of thumb, listeners can rarely attend for more minutes than their age. So limit teacher talk time. In fact, in this world of endless distraction, cut the age limit in half and use it as a guide for how long to perform as Sage on the Stage. This means, for an average twelve-year-old limit talk to no more than six minutes!

At the end of the six minutes, students can stop and jot: writing down a summary of what they heard. Then provide time to share the writing with a neighbor. Both students can then adjust their notes to reflect anything they heard from their partner that they missed on their own. Finally, you can challenge the class to nominate "the best summary they heard" to be read for everyone. All students can then adjust their notes to add ideas or correct misinformation.

Then begin the cycle again. To get information into long-term memory, students can share notes at the beginning of class on the following day to review and clarify learning.

Activity #2: Respond to Reading

Textbooks at the secondary level are often abandoned when we feel our students cannot handle the reading. In good faith efforts, teachers find it more expedient to tell information to students. This does a disservice to students who are challenged because they never get any reading practice. For them, reading tasks are avoided for much of the day. Textbooks and lecture are two alternative ways to transmit the same organized knowledge in any content.

Because many students struggle with reading, supporting the reading can advance reading skills while learning the content. Rather than assigning textbook reading for homework, assign it for in-class reading. Teach students to survey the reading and then predict, in writing, what they think they will be reading about. Break the reading up, and have students reevaluate their prediction and make a new one (see Montaigne's *Essai* in Chapter 5 for a step-by-step plan). Students can share their responses to the reading in small groups, by using reading responses as described in Chapter 4. Note making can become a group process as students "harvest" others' ideas and incorporate them into their own notebooks.

In Activities #1 and #2, note the number of times students are exposed to the content material in recursive activities. Not only are we teaching content, we are teaching the underlying processes which support learning and can be used throughout life.

Activity #3: Letter Writing

To review and coalesce knowledge, have students explain concepts in a letter to someone else. This could be a mythical person like *Princess Elsa* or a real person like *your grandmother*. Or have a student in one class write to a student in another class. The advantage of this method is that the writer has the hope of a response where any missing information can be filled in by the respondent. (If students are feeling threatened, assign a number to each student so they can remain anonymous. Students are paired by number.) Ask students to explain a concept to a younger student to gauge their real understanding. Translating knowledge into broad concepts for a younger group shows deep understanding.

Here's an easy way to incorporate letter writing into your classes while letting the students do much of the work for you. Gather enough spiral or composition books for a class set. Number each notebook. Assign each student in every class a number. Students will anonymously correspond with all other numbered students in each class. For instance, #12 in period one will be writing to #12 in all other periods. Students can write a letter describing lessons, asking questions about content, sharing news related to the unit, or any number of other course-related concepts. Students in subsequent classes can respond in writing and then add their own thoughts. These become supportive pen pals throughout the semester. For fun, have a pen pal party at the end of the course where the students can meet each other. Of course, this can be recreated digitally in a protected blogging space that spans all enrolled students; however, the novelty of writing a letter may appeal to our digitally flooded students.

Activity #4: Class Minutes as a Class Daybook
Assign a different student each day to keep track of the activities of the class for absentees. The notebook remains in the room for access by those who missed class. The minutes can be read (or not) at the beginning of each class as a review. Encourage students to include all the "social" activities that occur in the day as well—like jokes made—to build a community of learners.

Writing to Transform Knowledge
A great deal of understanding can be gained from transforming information from expository facts into another form. These activities get at the highest level of Bloom's taxonomy where students are afforded the opportunity to create, evaluate, and analyze, thus constructing knowledge and transforming it into another product.

There are a few ways to transform content into a new form to help students both show their understanding and to remember the concepts and information. These are common writing-across-the-curriculum activities which can be done more frequently if they are a part of a Daybook and shared more casually rather than assigned for high-stakes summative assessments. Provide them so students have ample opportunity to think their way through content before assessing it formally.

Activity #5: Dialogues

Students can create a dialogue between two historical figures, two math concepts or symbols, two biological functions or body parts, etc. The dialogues are fun when shared. The activity forces students to anthropomorphize the idea and must feature the basic characteristics.

Activity #6: Bio-Poem

Students follow a set formula to write the biography of an item under consideration. This can be a real person or complex terms or concepts like *manifest destiny* or *imaginary numbers*. Here is the format:

Bio-Poem

Line 1: Name the person, term, or concept.
Line 2: Provide four traits that describe the character, term, or concept.
Line 3: Related to . . .
Line 4: Lover of . . .
Line 5: Who (or which) feels . . . (three items)
Line 6: Who (or which) needs . . . (three items)
Line 7: Who (or which) fears . . . (three items)
Line 8: Who (or which) gives . . . (three items)
Line 9: Who (or which) would like to see . . . (three items)
Line 10: Resident of . . .
Line 11: Last name or a synonym of the term or concept.

Activity #7: Creative Definitions

Ask students to write their own definitions for new words. Students decide if the definition is factual or fictional. Follow up by providing a real definition.

Activity #8: Journal Entries

Create a journal entry for a day written in the voice of a person, term, or concept. For example, as students to write about "A Day in the Life of an Equal Sign."

Activity #9: Scenario

Create a plot for what might occur surrounding an historic event or a concept from a unit. For example, what might an organism experience during mitosis?

Activity #10: RAFT Writing

This handy graphic organizer can be used repeatedly in the content area to get students looking at concepts and ideas through different lenses (see Figure 6.2). RAFT stands for Role, Audience, Format, Topic. In a content class, the teacher can choose the topic or students can fill in as many topics as they recall from a unit and use the sheet to review a unit.

Then in small groups or as a class have students brainstorm the other columns. Come up with as many scenarios as possible so students have an opportunity to choose among the writing situations. Once they've chosen one, get them writing in the Daybook, sharing, acting out parts, and reviewing the unit.

Figure 6.2 A completed RAFT chart for an Earth Science course.

Role	Audience	Format	Topic
Volcano	Island	Announcement	Forming land mass
Sea	Volcano	Love letter	Forming land mass
Islanders	Volcano	Rap song	Forming land mass
Earthquake	Volcano	Persuasive essay	Who's better at forming land mass
Magma	Shifting plates	Song	Forming land mass

Activity #11: Completions

Provide an open-ended sentence that students can complete in as many ways as possible. "An alternative to the Declaration of Independence would be . . ."

Activity #12: Prewrite Questions or Conclusions

In looking at Adler's chart (page 92), it is noted that socratic seminars are opportunities for discussions of large ideas and values surrounding the content. It has been my experience that all students relish the opportunity to consider the differing points of view of their peers. Prior to discussions, provide students with writing think time to flesh out what they might want to bring to a discussion fraught with issues. Use the prewrite as an entry ticket into seminars. Students who have not done the prewrite cannot join the seminar but can still earn minimal participation points by exhibiting engagement through note making. Following a Socratic discussion, provide writing time so students can collect their thoughts around the discussion. An easy prompt is to ask "How has our talking today made a difference? Explain what primary idea you are taking with you." (See the Seminar handouts and directions in Appendix B.)

The above activities give the student another opportunity to make the learning their own by manipulating language in the context of new learning. To make the writings immediately useful they can share with students or sit in an author's chair and share with the whole class. Students should hear what others wrote as another opportunity to correct or expand their own understanding of concepts and information. Additional prompting for content area classes can be found by searching for writing prompts along with your content area: *writing prompts and math*, for example. If you are using a Daybook for these exploratory writings, write-to-learn activities can be offered more frequently and shared on the spot. Grading and rubrics do not need to be developed if participation is the only criteria assessed. Students can choose one to develop for a summative assessment that shows what they learned if you are using the Daybook to develop assignments. Students can choose from among the regular, exploratory writings to show what they know.

Prompting to Access English Classroom Concepts—With Application in Other Content

Over the years, I have amassed many prompts especially helpful at accessing underlying concepts in the English classroom. Though these are primarily focused on skill development in a reading, writing, speaking, and listening course, these literate behaviors are needed in the content area. Remember that students will not automatically transfer these skills to other content. To some degree, we have brought this problem on ourselves by dissecting knowledge into separate disciplines. But with philosophical argument aside, even in my English classroom, the concepts must be continually reinforced with each new thinking problem since most students are not developmentally ready to transfer skills to a new content without some instructional support. Students need reminders that one process will bleed into the next literacy challenge. This is likely to extend well into early adulthood when the brain has finally knit together accumulated skill building and we see easy transference of skill and knowledge (Willingham 2009).

Adaptations of these English arts concepts are offered for content use. These are lessons where the central focus is on a writing activity which reveals a concept. The writing is incidental to the learning and is not collected or graded. If content teachers intend to ask students to write, the lessons help students absorb and own new material.

Lesson #1: Show Versus Tell to Teach Good Writing *and* Good Reading

Even my Advanced Placement seniors look at me strangely when I ask them what we learn about a character, the mood, or the tone of a situation from a descriptive passage. Inference, or drawing conclusions from details, often seems like a made-up game, even though, as I point out to students, they participate in this kind of inferencing regularly in their daily lives. There's something about transferring the skill to investigating text which stymies students. Likewise, the old writing canard of "show me, don't tell me" is easy to say, but much harder to produce.

First draft writing of stories, poems, and argumentative essays are often full of *telling*. Even accomplished writers admit that most first drafts are "crap" (Ernest Hemingway, Anne Lamott, and Stephen King to name a few). Good writing happens in revisions of the first draft. Students need to understand this, but so should teachers in all disciplines. It is likely that, without supports in getting through a process that refines thinking until it attains the level of clear prose, many students are turning in first draft writing. And even if a first draft is coherent, without using the technique of *showing*, prose is lifeless and uninteresting.

Showing vs. telling and drawing inferences are two sides of the same language coin: we draw inferences from details when we read; we create mood, tone, and character by showing those details when we write. In non-fiction, argumentative, and informal writing, multiple examples *show* a concept that the author is trying to *tell* us about.

The following is a Daybook activity effective in all levels of the English classroom to demonstrate the difference between *showing* and *telling*. My students arrive at the application of this skill at various stages throughout the year and must always be reminded to turn first draft *telling* into final draft *showing*. The inverse of the lesson has us looking at what authors are *showing* so we can draw our own inference as we read.

Use this lesson early in the year to help students develop their writing skills while improving their close-reading analysis. Once the basic idea is presented, students can be reminded, "You're doing a lot of telling here. Is there something you can show to get your point across?" In reading, return to the initial lesson by asking students what is the author trying to *tell* us through this descriptive *showing* passage.

I begin by using my own life experience as a model. I recommend all teachers do the same: model for your students with a real event from your own life. Tell your stories to the class. They love hearing about you. The modeling confirms that good ideas come from experience, and we can use our experiences as a reliable foundation on which to build new learning. If you bring your experiences into the room it will encourage students to do the same. A bonus is all the insider knowledge we gain about our students and their previous successes and struggles.

Create your own telling and showing passages like the one modeled below and use those stories with your students.

First I write on the board:

My brother is gross.

Then below that I write:

One evening at dinner my brother stopped all conversation by picking up a paper napkin, sopping up the gravy on his plate, and sticking it in his mouth to suck out the juices.

This is not high literature, but it is effective in making a point. The first sentence *tells* the reader that my brother is gross. The second *shows* a real experience. Hopefully anyone who reads the second sentence would draw his own conclusion—*ick!*—and there would be no need for the first.

Students are then directed to write their own telling sentence. They should choose a real person or a pet because those images are easy to access. They can write their telling sentence by connecting a subject with a predicate adjective using the *to be* verb. This is the general pattern of a telling sentence, and a very brief grammar lesson can reinforce the pattern. Point out the subject, the predicate adjective, and then remind students of the variations on *to be*, our most irregular verb (is, was, were, am, will be, etc.). Later students can use this sentence pattern to locate their own *telling* sentences.

My (*subject*) is (*predicate adjective*).

After writing the *telling* sentence, students should write a *showing* passage on another page where a reader cannot see the telling sentence. Again, if students use real experiences, they will find this writing easy. They need only think of an example of the trait they are trying to express. Remind students that their predicate adjective (in my case, the word *gross*) should not appear anywhere in their showing passage.

Generally, struggling students find this fun and easy to do, especially if the person or pet chosen is *crazy* or *hilarious*. In fact, the most outrageous examples generally come from struggling students, and they feel a great sense of accomplishment if they can entertain their peers with their example. My own example is deliberately outrageous (for a teacher anyway) to give students permission to write the truth of their lives—often considered not-for-school topics.

After writing, students partner up and read each other's showing passages. Without seeing the original telling sentence, the reading partner must guess it. When a reading partner guesses—or comes close to guessing the telling sentence, the writer "wins." They have successfully shown a character trait without naming it. This is always a fun class activity and many students volunteer to share their showing passages so the rest of the class can guess the telling sentence.

Of course, the reader/listeners are merely drawing an inference. When students see that most readers draw a similar conclusion to the showing passage, we are getting an inside-out view of both author's craft and close reading. The "trick" of inferring is no longer a trick; it is based on combining our own life experiences with the text. Authors who craft these descriptions are no longer invisible magicians, but the students who sit beside us. A side benefit is that students who "win" by succeeding in affecting their readers emotionally begin to see that there is some power in their own writing drawn from experience. This lesson has had deep resonance with the non-traditional student, the one least likely to be considered a *writer*.

To reinforce this exercise take it in two directions.

◆ Pull some descriptive passages from the current reading. Have students guess the *telling sentence* the author intended. With a simple change of wording—*What is the author trying to* tell *us through this* showing?—students shift their inferencing skills to the class text. If you are working on analysis, students can write a paragraph explaining the effect of the description intended by the author. If you are working in a content area, ask students which concept is being exemplified through the examples. Be sure students include the details that helped them understand what the author was trying to *tell*.

◆ Have students examine their own writing for telling sentences. Remind students that telling sentences usually have some variation of the verb *to be*. Students can start by highlighting all the various *to be* verbs in their writing. Have students choose one or two telling sentences that can be shown rather than told. Ask them to move the *telling* sentence to a new page and then write the *showing*. This is deep revision at practice.

◆ Students might also choose to use the showing and telling exercise as the start of a character (or pet) sketch.

Lesson #2: Examining Metaphors and Symbols Through Creative Writing

Nothing is more daunting in the language arts classroom than understanding both the complexity that metaphors bring to poetry and prose as well as the concept that concrete objects and experiences serve to deliver the abstractions of theme, tone, and mood. T.S. Eliot called this the objective correlative, the idea that authors find a set of objects, a situation, or a chain of events to embody ideas.

This Daybook activity is an introduction to several concepts in the English classroom: the difference between concrete and abstract nouns, understanding metaphor and symbol, and supporting concepts for the development of a thesis statement. It's a tall order to fill but the activity is fun, accessible, and shows the inside-out of writer's craft. Students remember this lesson partly, I think, because of the elements of surprise and exploration.

First, students must get out a sheet of notebook paper and fold it lengthwise (hot dog style). On the left-hand side of the page (with the page still folded) the students list twenty concrete nouns. Now is the time to teach, or reteach, the definition of a concrete noun: the name of something that can be physically accessed through the senses. In a content course, adapt this to require that students list the names of "things" presented in the course: integers, mitochondria, parallelograms, laws, specific historical documents, and so forth.

Secondly, students flip the folded page over so they cannot see the original list and, beginning on the same line they began the list of concrete nouns, they list twenty abstractions: the names of ideas or feelings that can neither be seen nor touched (like *love, patriotism, loneliness,* and so forth). This list is harder for students to develop so a lot of sharing, calling out, and searching the posters of the room for abstractions is generally part of the list making. Remember to help students access the vocabulary they need whenever possible. Using new vocabulary repeatedly is the best way to pull those words into a student's verbal and written production.

Abstractions are, of course, often themes in novels; but students must first understand how both concrete experiences and even objects can do the heavy lifting of carrying the experience of an abstraction from one human being to another (Eliot's thesis). Making the invisible visible is the task of any author who dares to translate the human experience. Gaining the language to express the implied abstraction that an author delivers, either through poetry, prose, or drama, is the task of analysis.

It is a difficult leap for many students to grasp what is being implied by the physical. Making this connection from one human being to another—a kind of *Do you see and feel what I see and feel?*—is the chief aim of art. This exercise in writing and thinking helps students see how we often connect the physical to the metaphysical.

After students create their two lists with concrete nouns on the left-hand side of the page and abstractions on the right, they open the page and write the word *of* between the two nouns. Immediately students see that they now have a phrase of incongruities like *the pencil of loneliness* or *the coffee cup of patriotism*.

The connection of a physical object to a metaphysical idea generally delights the entire class, and they begin to laugh in surprise when two seemingly disparate nouns are now connected. Spontaneous sharing—*Listen to this one!*—begins as students discover an otherwise unlikely combination as quirky or delightful.

The final direction asks students to circle their five or six favorite combinations, or just the ones that challenge, delight, or puzzle them. The human mind being what it is, students sense a kind of meaning in the nonsense. Most students tend toward the most divergent, eliminating the obvious like *bed of love* or *coffee cup of anxiety*.

This new list of favorite combinations is transferred into the Daybook and students choose one as a prompt for a daily writing in whatever way they see fit: as a poem, a short story, a rumination on how the object and the idea are connected. Students in the past have used the phrase for lyrics to a song, the beginning of a poem, the central focus of a short story, or—my favorite—the name of their band. In every case, students craft a piece that reveals the abstraction through the object.

The lesson is not lost on most students: we can root the metaphysical in the physical. This can be backed up with short reminders of the many, many physical reminders of ideas in our everyday life. The American flag that hangs in every classroom is a good starting point. I ask students what abstractions are represented in the physical flag. *Does it carry the same idea for every group who sees it? What other ideas does it represent? What does it mean to you? How are those meanings related to your experiences? Will every symbol carry the same meaning for everyone?*

In fact, communicating our invisible experiences *must* be rooted in the concrete or else we have no other way of sharing them with our fellow human beings. The use of metaphor is as old as language. This exercise merely amplifies our tendency to see connections and share them with others through our everyday comparisons.

The concrete/abstract noun writing exercise also sets the groundwork for later discussions on theme and author's purpose in a literature course. Their list of twenty abstractions is also a list of twenty potential themes. Students are shown how to develop a thesis statement by identifying an abstraction that they determine is central to the work. The student's next task is to justify the author's comment on the abstraction. For instance, most students can identify a poem with *love* as its central focus but must think more deeply in determining what comment the author is making on the idea of love: Is it the transcendence of love beyond life? Is it the enduring nature of love? Is it love's ability to transform the lover's world? These questions will require that the student return to the concrete in the poem or prose to determine what aspect of the abstraction the author is exploring. His or her choice of comparative language will be key to understanding the author's commentary.

Ideally, students will be working with some text that contains metaphors and we can connect the abstract/concrete lesson to the text by finding and unpacking the metaphor. *What idea is being connected to which object? Why? What qualities does the object have that the author is trying reveal in the abstraction?* This analysis is difficult for many students but the prompt and student writing help them see how the language is providing nuance and depth to the text.

The concrete/abstract exercise is just a beginning point to recognize what might be implied by a literary text. After choosing a favorite phrase from the concrete/abstract lists, the writing portion of the activity shows the student how an author can develop an object or experience into carrying an idea. To challenge students, ask that they use the object in a passage that suggests the abstraction without naming it. The exercise reveals how the subconscious creates symbols by returning to them repeatedly in the act of creating art. Analysis is easier when students begin to see both the human thought and the craft behind the writing in this exercise.

Lesson #3: Another Approach at Metaphor—Through a Poem as Extended Metaphor

Help students understand how extended metaphor works in a poem by having students create a metaphor-based poem of their own. Take them through the following steps.

- List ten specific things from nature. Rather than trees, name oak trees. Rather than flowers, say daffodils.
- List five people, family members and friends. (For content writing, have students choose important ideas from the unit.)
- Choose an item (or a term from the unit) and then someone you know who is like that item.
- List ways in which they are similar.
- Then, write a poem in which you describe the item when in reality you are describing the person or term. Do not name or refer to the person or content term in the poem.

Lesson #4: Twenty Events—Listing for Topics

This is a simple Daybook activity that can be done several times during a course to develop the observational skills of an author in the English classroom. Content area teachers can adapt the twenty events list to ask students to list and then note where in their day they believe they are impacted by science, or math, or art, or physical fitness, or health choices.

Ask students to review the past twenty-four hours and list twenty events they participated in during the time (waking up, showering, traveling to school, etc.). After listing, have students circle or identify two or three they feel they would want to write about. In the content area, the directions here would be more specific. For instance, have students scan the list looking for a place where their daily interactions intersect with an argument in the wider world, or are impacted by the discoveries of science, or have an element of mathematical reasoning imbedded in them, and so on. They should select these intersections for listing.

Then ask them to choose one that makes them want to write. Set a timer and have them write about that specific action in this past twenty-four hours, observing and responding to the event in the context of your framing question. This is how a writer lives his or her life: mining experience for writing. Students sit in the author's chair and write from one of their own life experiences listed in the twenty events. This is also an opportunity to open your content course to specific student interactions with the subject. Rather than providing a teacher view of the content in the real world, we can get students focusing on this intersection on their own and sharing that with others. If students have not seen where the content intersects their lives, this should help.

One year a student declared in his end of course reflection (see Chapter 8): "I've learned that *anything* can be the topic for writing." This may seem like a "duh" moment, but if all school writing has been either assigned or tested writing, then this is something of an epiphany.

The twenty events list can be used to develop a "Slice of Life" essay (see Chapter 5, page 83) where the student observes and comments on their event, or an essay on how a discipline shapes or affects a life.

Lesson #5: Practicing Imagery

This prompt can be done repeatedly to help students understand theme, mood, and tone. There is never too much practice with these concepts since many students come to understand them at different developmental points. The exercise is like "show, don't tell" where students are invited to show rather than name a theme.

The prompt for any of these writings is the same, but the abstraction can be changed to whatever you want students to show through images. This is a good anticipatory activity when introducing a new work. Use the themes you expect them to encounter in the text.

Imagine you are making a movie and need five minutes of silent film that conveys the idea of loneliness. *What will you show? What kind of lighting and images will be on screen? Who will be the main character? What angles will you use?*

Change *loneliness* to *isolation* or *community* or *alienation*—any theme will do. Students can see, again, how description leads to inference—another "inside-out" view of writer's craft. But being able to infer is the chief tool of historians, scientists, and mathematicians too. Because our students are expert consumers of images, this is usually a prompt that inspires confidence. In my co-taught special education classes, students have shown immense pride in sharing their written images. These have been the most memorable responses to this activity.

Lesson #6: Teaching Archetype Through Personal Experience

Literary analysis can be a puzzle for some students. Teaching the archetypes of story as a psychological, metaphorical mirror can help students understand how story operates on several levels.

To introduce the idea of archetypes and symbolism, take students through a guided visualization for both *fear* and *peace*. A guided visualization asks students to sit with their eyes closed while you orally *walk* them through an imaginary place. (See the *Back in the Real World* feature for a script.) After the guided visualization, ask them to list the images brought to mind.

Back in the Real World

Guided visualizations have often been used by sports psychologists to help athletes envision and project their own success. We can borrow this technique to help students better understand archetypal images. Students can do the visualization either with their eyes open or closed, and then should write to capture the images; or you can guide them with your voice as they record images.

Imagine you are entering an area where you experience great [fear/peace/relaxation]: Where are you? What do you see in the environment? What colors dominate? Is there an object, animal, or person? What do they look like? What smells are around you? What can you hear? Can you feel anything? Is there any air moving? What does it feel like? What sensations are you experiencing?

 Teacher Tip

Take students through a relaxation visualization prior to a test or other anxiety-producing school experience. Students can focus on relaxing images to reduce stress.

In the large group, collect the images that came to mind by recording them on the board and see how many overlap among the students. Explain that this is the Jungian theory that the human subconscious has a shared store of images we associate with certain ideas and emotions. His theory is that we all respond similarly to certain visual or experiential images and this is the basis for many of the archetypes used by authors when transmitting human emotion in art. Students can then be introduced to these archetypal images and how they appear in our art (prose, poetry, movies, music).

After teaching the archetypes, prompt students to see the connection to human experience by asking them to apply the archetypes to their own lives. I use the prompts below in parallel with whatever literature we are working on to reveal how the microcosm of a text is amplifying the macrocosm of the universe.

After asking students to write on one and how it appears in their lives, have them transfer the question to the work under study (i.e. In *Grendel*, what quest is the monster on?). The answers to the questions can be a pre-discussion think/write to help students engage each other with the large ideas in the text. Supporting their archetype with quotes would be a natural next step.

The Archetype Questions: (also good for seniors starting college essays or for self-exploration):

◆ Write about a quest or journey of discovery on which you have embarked.
◆ Tell about a time you went outside your known realm, a story of exploration that could be physical or intellectual.
◆ Write about dragons you've slain.
◆ Write about initiations you have undergone, times when you have gone from innocence to experience, child to adult, dependent to independent.
◆ Give an account of an apprenticeship you've served with a mentor or master teacher, including telling about when you had to venture out on your own to employ the lessons and skills they'd taught.
◆ Write about a talismanic object in your life, some physical artifact that invests your life with meaning and power.
◆ Tell a transformation story about a time you changed: your looks, your mind, your environment, your friends, your attitude, your direction.
◆ Write about honor in terms of a time when you had to uphold your own highest, chivalric ideals.
◆ Jot down some thoughts about your heroes in life. What have been their quests, setbacks, temptations, victories? Do they fit the archetypal heroic mold? How do your modern-day heroes differ from traditional archetypal heroes? What do any differences communicate about our present-day society?

The focus of these prompts centers on self-evaluation and a recognition of and subsequent codification of student values and traits. Besides being engaging, and revealing the course objective of connecting the hero's journey to our own, the thinking-in-writing time is important in the formation of the self. We are, after all, the hero in our own ongoing narrative.

To adapt the archetypes to content area writing, ask students to identify an historically significant person in the content and outline their hero's journey using the above questions for the historical figure (or the development of an organism or continent) rather than themselves. Story is a powerful tool for condensing information. If students can create a story around their learning they are more likely to recall it.

Lesson #7: Ten Wonderful Things—Writing With Specificity and Building Experience With Microcosm/Macrocosm

Set a timer for seven minutes and challenge students to write a list of ten wonderful things. Model the idea of what constitutes a *wonderful thing* for them because they must understand that they cannot write in generalities (*kittens*). They must write very specific instances of something wonderful (*When you hit green lights at all the stops on Route 50 heading east out of town*).

Sharing is a *must* after this writing so forewarn students that there will be sharing. Done early in the year this is a great community builder. Your *wonderful thing* is usually someone else's as well. During sharing, there is a lot of smiling, laughing, *ahs*, and head nodding. The activity reinforces the idea that we aren't all that different from each other and can experience the same joy from minute, ordinary experience. This is one of my absolute favorite activities because we all feel good for the rest of the day.

The details can lead to a microcosm/macrocosm discussion of the ability of humans to see themselves reflected in a shared, specific experience. My students are reminded that if they write the details of their lives fully, we will see our own experiences in those details.

Here are some student examples of *wonderful things* we all celebrated with that knowing *Ah!* from the whole class:

- ◆ "When one pump on the ketchup dispenser at Burger King fills the plastic cup to the brim."
- ◆ "The straight lines left in the carpet after vacuuming."
- ◆ "Not knowing it was going to snow and waking up to find out school is canceled."

Here is a wonderful thing from Amy Krouse Rosenthal's *Encyclopedia of an Ordinary Life* (2005). (She has many examples in this quirky, unique memoir/autobiography that can inspire student writing. The book resembles Daybook ruminations sorted and categorized by the alphabet.) Under the entry "French Fries": "How great is it to find a few stray bonus fries at the bottom of your McDonald's bag?" (105).

Since students are expected to also write at home, suggest that at least some of their entries—maybe once a week—include time to reflect with gratitude for all that is going right in their world. Besides being a positive, reflective writing, students can begin to build a store of resilience by thinking about their lives from the positive side of the balance sheet. This flips the usual deficit model—where we only measure what is *not* working—found in most school experience.

Students can pull one of the wonderful things from their list for an extended Daybook entry. The list forms its own set of prompts when students are looking for inspiration.

To extend the "Wonderful Things" exercise into the content areas, ask students to list three to five *wonderful things* that a volcano might consider great, or Franklin Roosevelt, or the Piedmont of Virginia. Personifying aspects of any curriculum helps students build strong connections to the material (and have fun).

Lesson #8: Ten Annoying Things—More Details That Move Into Argument or Problem Solving

Later in the year repeat the above exercise, only this time use *ten annoying things*. This writing should follow the same as the example above: model, write a list for seven minutes, share, and choose one to write about.

Though this does not produce the same feel-good response as the *ten wonderful things*, annoying things can become the basis of an argumentative essay or deeper research question. Students can discuss what's behind the "annoying thing" and whether there is anything that can be done to eliminate the annoyance. This list can become fodder for a student's own curiosity and can be a first step in developing a personal inquiry in any subject area.

One year the students unanimously listed *No more homemade cookies at lunch* as a widely shared *annoying thing*. Behind this annoyance students were prompted to find out why they were no longer getting the warm homemade cookies they cherished. This revealed to them the complex web of regulations that a school cafeteria labors under (who knew!). The handicapped students in the building had been making the cookies and had run afoul of some regulation. Rather than go through the paperwork and upgrades needed to comply, the program had to be dropped. This was a long lesson in learning how the small things in our lives can be affected by larger decisions made at a distance. Students who learn this lesson early in life will become active citizens who seek out solutions to commonplace annoyances. One of our daily annoyances may become a passionate exercise in reform.

A variation on "Ten Annoying Things" is to ask students to generate a list of "Things You Worry About." This list can help students locate research projects and potentially relieve their own worry. When we share these lists, I tell students to make a complete list, but only share the ones they feel comfortable sharing. Students bring a lot of worries to school from home situations they might not want to make public. When the large group shares, our students reveal that they are often worried about many of the same things. This is another opportunity to build a culture of community in the classroom.

Lesson #9: Short Words

Sometimes our students believe that good writing means using an impressively large vocabulary. Remind students that we want to *write to express, not to impress*. This activity is a powerful reminder that we can do a lot with short words and need not rely on impressive words which often wring the voice out of writing.

First, I read aloud the chapter "The Case for Short Words" by Richard Lederer out loud while students follow along. In it he argues that there is much power in using small, sometimes very old words. Lederer is a syndicated columnist and author of over thirty books on often playful aspects of English. The entire chapter is easily accessible on the Internet.

After reading the chapter together, the class is challenged to write in the Daybook using only one-syllable words. Several topics are provided to help students who may be stuck. Sharing reveals that students can compose powerful, image-laden writing with small words—and in a short amount of time.

Lesson #10: The Power of Verbs

In the showing vs. telling activity we begin locating the weakest but most common of the verbs: the *to be* verb. In a later assignment, I show students how images are often carried through the verbs.

Here is a Daybook prompt which can help students see how verbs can build an image:

Students fold a paper vertically in half ("hot dog style"). With the paper folded, students list verbs used in cooking. We shout out ideas and share until they come up with at least ten (sauté, boil, frappe, slice, blend, etc.). Then students flip the folded paper over and list ten things you see at the beach (crabs, children, seagulls, etc.).

With the paper unfolded, have students experiment with sentences that describe the beach using the verbs with the things you see at the beach. Challenge students to come up with a descriptive paragraph. This begins the student awareness of looking for unusual verbs in their reading and writing.

Example paragraph: Seagulls boil around the French fries at the edge of the water, unnoticed by knots of children stirring water and sand into castles downwind. The wind folds towels and belongings into piles of gritty architecture. The mid-afternoon sun fries office-white skin into the pink flag of "my vacation."

Use this as a revision activity while students are working on a draft. If students are working on an academic paper, provide a list (see Appendix C) of replacement verbs for commonly used ones like *said* and *use*. These will add specificity and a tone of confidence to academic writing.

Poetry Prompting

In my poetry unit, the students write a poem each day in their Daybooks. I call this Daybook Poetry. None of the poems are collected or graded, though students share every day in class.

The purpose of the daily poetry writing is to get students trying out author's craft. The daily sharing, first with a partner and then by election (*Who would like to volunteer someone who will read for us?*) elevates the student to author. Classroom feedback is always positive since poems are always met with the poetry snapping endemic of a coffee house. At the end of the course, a fair number of students claim to both enjoy and better understand poetry. Many students choose to develop one or more of their poems in their personal writing (see Appendix C for this assignment). Some even take it on as a new favorite genre for writing. Poems also appear regularly in the selected best works of the end of course Portfolio. These outcomes are achieved without grades. Our sharing from the author's chair is always celebratory. One year I used a gold star-shaped sticky note declaring *I'm a Poet!* for students to wear all day when they took the risk of sharing their seven-minute works of art.

Here are some prompts which work especially well.

Lesson #11: In Response to a News Event—Poetic Distance

After reading two poems which were inspired by actual news events, "Norman Morrison" by Adrian Mitchell and "Out, Out" by Robert Frost, students are invited to find a recent news event and write a poem in response to it. In the Norman Morrison poem, a specific event is referenced in great specific detail to make a pointed political statement about the Vietnam War. In Frost's poem, though based on a specific event, the speaker generalizes the event of the death of a boy. His poem touches on the more universal tragedy of a child's death. After writing, the poems are shared. Students identify the news event after hearing the poem or indicate whether the student poet has distanced him or herself from the event. In this manner, poetic distance is understood as a reader but also as a device deliberately chosen by a writer to achieve a specific effect.

Lesson #12: Synecdoche

Students are invited to enter a poem through a body part. First, play Bill Withers's blues song "Grandma's Hands" as a model. Then ask students to think of a person, or persons, who is important to them. Students are encouraged to choose one of the people and focus on a physical aspect of their being to use as a repetitive feature of the poem just as Withers uses the hands of his grandmother.

Lesson #13: Working With Sound

Provide a list of interesting-sounding words. Challenge students to use at least five of the words in a poem. Here is an example of words which could be used: *flim flam, knick knack, flip flop, willy nilly, rick rack, bric-a-brac, rip rap,* and so on.

Lesson #14: iPod Poetry (Found Poetry)

Students are especially surprised by the results of this activity. Have students open the device they store their music on. Have them arrange song titles into a poem. For students who do not have a device, keep a few magazines or newspapers on hand for the old standard method of creating found poetry—pulling words from text. Have students scavenge for phrases to combine into poetry. In a room full of teenagers immersed in music, this activity brings out many who are willing to share.

Lesson #15: Fortune Cookie Poetry

If you're willing to invest in some fortune cookies, or can get a restaurant to donate, hand out the cookies and have students incorporate their fortune into a poem.

Lesson #16: Strength/Weakness Poem

List your strengths and then your weaknesses. Create two characters: one for the strengths and one for the weaknesses. Create a dialogue between the two. This could result in a poem for two voices.

Lesson #17: Teaching Irony

List ten bad habits. Choose one. Write a poem where each line begins with *Praise* or *Bless* and then follow it with a quality or action of the bad habit.

Or try an apology poem modeled after William Carlos Williams's "This Is Just to Say" in which the speaker apologizes for something they have no remorse for.

There are many poetry exercises available to English teachers from a variety of resources. These do not need to be held back for a single grading opportunity. In any subject, we can build confidence in our students by immersing them in practice tied to strong models until the genre is familiar enough that the student feels some mastery. By using the safe space of the Daybook, you can let students try and try again until they are willing to assume the risk of evaluation. In our classroom, many of these poems were immediately "published" as students shared them with peers and then were elected for a reading in the author's chair. Many poets were born through regular Daybook poetry.

Summing Up

Writing can be incorporated into classrooms and simultaneously fulfill our curricular goals. Shifting to writing to replace other traditional teacher behaviors moves the students into a discovery role. Begin by experimenting with writing within a unit and then expand your repertoire of writing tools to give students an insider's view of content.

For the Daybook, Incorporate the Following:

◆ Build in a stop-and-write session when lecture is necessary. Students should transform information into their own words, rather than copying notes. Student sharing fills in gaps and confirms basic understanding.

◆ Bring literate behaviors in by letting students read textbooks and other relevant material in class. Sharing of note making in pairs and with the large group codifies the important organized knowledge.

◆ Let students manipulate new information through playful writing exercises.

◆ Employ writing exercises that simultaneously teach or review material.

◆ Build in sharing time to create consensus around ideas and a community of learners.

The next chapter shows how to use the Daybook to support students in developing writing that results in a summative assessment—like essays or reports.

7

Why Are These Essays So Hard to Read?

Scaffolding Student Products by Collecting and Brainstorming Before Assigning

"Don't waste time waiting for inspiration. Begin, and inspiration will find you."

—H. Jackson Brown, Jr.

What to Expect

This chapter introduces activities and formats for supporting students in writing summative papers. The Daybook can encourage students to think about topics over time and can serve to collect observations and inquiry questions for end-of-unit or course writing assessments. Students need this support so they can write with confidence. The better a student understands a topic, the clearer the writing will be. While our students are developing their written communication skills, we need to support a process that reflects and teaches how real writers work.

Chapter Topics

◆ Understanding the difference between assigning and supporting writing.
◆ Creating opportunities for students to explore and collect ideas.
◆ Breaking through writing blocks to get started and to identify gaps for research.
◆ Identifying gaps in research and argument.

But That's the Way We've Always Done It . . .

In my freshman year in college I received a typical assignment. We were required to compose an analytical paper on a piece of literature. Before we could begin our paper, we had to meet with the professor and have a thesis statement approved.

Spoiler alert: I cheated. I had no idea what I intended to say about the piece of literature assigned. So, I went to the library and read—a lot. I took notes, looked for patterns, and drew some conclusions. Finally, after several days of reading and note taking, I felt I had some grasp on an idea I could support with a level of confidence. I wrote it on a 3x5 card and met with my professor. The idea was approved, and I was granted permission to go ahead and write the paper. But, in essence, I had already done most of the writing, or at least the thinking and planning around the paper in advance of the approval. I could not come up with an idea until I had written and read and written again. We really *can't* know what we think until we see what we say.

Assigning Writing Versus Teaching Writing

Though that experience dates from 1973, teachers still make similar assignments: a teacher-created statement is offered for dissection, or one is demanded (a thesis statement), before a topic is approved. Students who understand that writing is about expressing ideas may follow my "cheating" model as a matter of course. Those who don't will follow the focus on form, creating a statement they know little about and then shoehorning quotes and other thoughts into some semblance of support. Still others will stumble around in half-formed thoughts, probably write something the night before it is due, not knowing where or how to begin because *they don't know what they are talking about*, but will likely conclude that they aren't very good at writing anyway.

What I learned from my hallway-fighting-Joey of Chapter 3 (page 46) was that it's my job to help students locate their ideas before writing so they can compose around those thoughts. In other words, I facilitate the location of pathways that lead to a centering on ideas in need of expression. This requires some time carved out of the classroom to provide students with tools for finding ideas. These opportunities can be relatively short in duration and practiced over a number of meetings before asking students to commit to a topic. Allowing students to choose topics is a strong support mechanism. Students will gravitate to subjects they feel some confidence in. This will subsequently improve the quality of the writing.

Writing to Collect for a Product

The largest complaint heard from non-English teachers is usually about the quality of student writing within assigned research papers. Non-English teachers are frustrated by tangled prose and the perceived inability to smoothly incorporate the voices of others into a paper.

Generally, many teachers are unaware of two truths about writing: every writing task is a new problem in thinking, but the skills practiced in English class will not naturally be transferred into another course; and *everyone* writes poorly when they do not know what they are writing about. These students have not learned how to "cheat" on a written product by doing a lot of thinking and reading around the topic.

To see more student success on content area written products, content area teachers can assist students by forcing some prewriting thinking in the Daybook before even beginning the research for the desired product.

Here are some examples of how to force the thinking before the research. Note that the first step is to offer natural, expressive writing opportunities. These first writings help push students through a block. They already have something down on paper—a *down draft*—now all they must do is fix it up—an *up draft*.

Activity #1: First Thoughts to Gather Student Knowledge Before Research

Students write or list their initial impressions about a topic they are about to explore. Prompt students to answer questions such as *What hunch do you have about . . .* or *What do you believe to be true about . . .* Or direct their thinking with some sentence stems: *I wish I could say in my paper that . . .* Or *What stands out to me after everything I've learned . . .* All the initial thoughts around the topic become a basis for inquiry to find out if what you believe to be true is in fact a truth or a fallacy. It is a great place to start research.

Activity #2: Facts, Lies, and Assumptions Before Researching

Start by writing a list about things you, and most of the students in the room, are sure are true about the question or topic. (This is the common knowledge aspect of many papers.)

Move on to listing or writing about things that you and everybody else seem to know are *not true* about the question or topic.

Finally move on to assumptions that you think might be true, or false, but you're not sure. Maybe you think they are not true, maybe they are: you are not sure. This is a great exercise in living with uncertainty. Our students rarely get the chance to live in this state, but it is the perfect jumping off place for true inquiry. If we acknowledge that there is this realm of uncertainty in any learning, by inviting it into our classrooms we are affirming an aspect of true thinking which is rarely celebrated. We want our students to recognize moments of uncertainty and capitalize on them as places to start real learning and questioning. Remembering, of course, that all of humanity has lived with this state of uncertainty for eons around some questions that remain unanswered.

Activity #3: Dialogues to Build Understanding of Audience

This exercise is very helpful in argument writing. The student assumes both sides of the conversation and writes in a dialogue format. This is also helpful in accessing thinking because thought tends more toward speech than formal essay. The fact that the student is writing a conversation also alleviates the pressure of adopting a scholarly tone.

To extend this further, have two students have a "silent conversation" around the topic. This provides a real-life rather than imagined foil for student argument. Direct students to fold a sheet of paper "hot dog style" (the long way). The controlling idea or topic is written across the top of the page.

One student begins by writing their initial idea, statement, or argument on the left and passes it to a partner. That student responds on the right with an opposing thought. The paper is passed back and forth between them as the conversation continues. The product is a listing of many views and ideas around the topic with many points that can be researched for supporting evidence. The writer will also have some sense of an opposing idea that must be addressed in a counter-argument.

Activity #4: Interruptions to Mimic How Real Writers Write

We can help students build effective writing by breaking our assignments into manageable parts. Assigning due dates to each phase, along with short, expressive writings, will help students write for meaning rather than tying together disconnected or nonsensical sources.

Due dates should reflect the process. Initially, students should present a topic or idea after writing over time in the Daybook. Then separate the research process into a searching, reading, and written response assignment. Writing logs are helpful for this. Only after reading and responding should students attempt a draft by using Activity #5.

Too often we expect students to do their researching and writing in tandem. This results in *patch writing*. Students select pertinent sentences from sources and string them together by changing a word here or there. The papers lack a flow and it is clear the student is not understanding the sources.

 Teacher Tip

Summarizing is a key skill that is often overlooked in its power to help students absorb material and monitor reading comprehension. Use this tool frequently. Challenge students to write $2 summing up sentences where every word is worth ten cents. Or collect thoughts in a 3–2–1 format: Three important ideas, two ideas for discussion or argument, one question.

Activity #5: If I Had to Write This Now . . . to Outrun the Judge

Ask students to pretend that they are writing a final draft of a paper about a certain subject. This instant version can help students clarify ideas and focus on bigger-picture thinking. Of course, this is low-risk writing because everyone knows the writing is being done long before they are ready. When working on a research paper, this writing should be done without access to notes or the research. The exercise helps students clarify what they already know or don't know about a subject. Additionally, they already have at least one draft of the paper, however limited it might be.

Back in the Real World

A typical student seven-minute version of an assigned character sketch after viewing Franco Zefferelli's *Hamlet*.

Students were given seven minutes to write the paper *if you had to write it now*. This student is writing her way to a thesis about Ophelia's general character traits, plus she touches on some interesting divergent thinking around Ophelia's perceived failures at the end of the time limit. This last line would make a great first line on a clean sheet of paper allowing the student to focus on the provocative idea. There is plenty to work with in this seven-minute down draft.

Ophelia's feelings throughout the play tend to be more negative. She is obedient to her father and the king and her brother. She is a little cautious and confused towards Hamlet. Overall I would describe Ophelia as childish. She still listens to her elders but she is still curious, and when she is not watched she tends to do the opposite of what she is told to do. She doesn't quite know what to do with Hamlet. There are mixed signals and she struggles between listening to what she has been told to do and following her whims. There are times that I was unsure if she knew what she was saying/ doing or if like a child she was merely copying what she had seen someone do or say.

Ophelia is especially childish in act IV when she goes mad. Her outward manner and the way she acts, how she sits in the chair with her legs curled up by her and hands out the flowers, is very childish. Her distachment [sic] from the ethereal world, and how she doesn't notice that she is in danger.

I think that Zeffirelli's version of Hamlet portrays Ophelia well. In the start she is extremely obedient, she is still curious towards Hamlet even when she is told to stay away. She seems to have a nice mix of both experienced yet young and nieve [sic]. Zeffirelli plays it out in a way that keeps you guessing. At least for me. I thought that some could have been like a child not knowing what she was saying—doing what she has seen. Ophelia is not pure but she is not a "whore"/ ruined girl. She is tainted. Taints are not pure but they can give way to new and beautiful things (in sense of colors—thought processes).

Activity #6: Devil's Advocate to Look for Holes in Thinking

After students have done some exploratory writings around their assigned topic, pair them with a student who will play the Devil's Advocate. The directions for the Devil's Advocate are to challenge every claim the student is making, without going easy on the student. If students are aware of the "game" they will not take offense. If the exercise is done in writing, like the dialogue in Activity #3, students will have a written record of new ideas or gaps in their understanding, perhaps because some of the time they were forced to respond *I don't know.* Otherwise students should keep notes on new ideas or knowledge gaps.

Reverse the roles so the other student has the benefit of going through their own topic under pressure.

Some good questions you can prep the Devil's Advocate with are:

How do you know that?
What's your evidence?
Have you thought about . . . [alternative solution]?
Point out places where the reasoning is poor.

In a general English class, my students were paired with interview partners after they had done a considerable amount of research. The partners had the student's original guiding questions for the project. Each person asked the other the questions and took notes on the answers in the graphic organizer (Appendix C) "Sample Check-In With Partner." The final column of the organizer is for information the student still must find. The sheets were returned to the author of the paper for further research and to organize writing, or in this case, speaking.

Activity #7: Narration to Turn Ideas Into Story

A scholarly paper can be a daunting problem. Even experienced writers face the same fears that our students have, wondering if this time they will be able to get their thoughts into clear focus. Switching the genre can help break through to the thinking and focus the piece. In this brainstorming exercise, shift the focus to a narrative writing. *What is the story of your thoughts around an idea? What happens first, next, and finally? Is there a climactic point?*

We're all familiar with story as an organizing feature. Getting thoughts out in story form first can help locate thinking and areas where more research is needed.

Activity #8: Cubing to Find Insight

This involves looking at a subject from several different views. Some instructors have students make an actual cube out of paper to emphasize that a subject is being turned over and looked at from a variety of angles. Others have students divide a paper into six squares and write within each square. Some of the cubing topics require divergent or figurative thinking. The different viewpoints are:

1. Describing: What does it look (smell, touch, taste) like? What are its parts?
2. Comparing: What is like this idea? What is different?
3. Association: What does this topic remind you of? Are there comparable experiences?
4. Analyzing: Break the topic into its parts. How are they related? Where did the topic come from? Where is it headed?
5. Applying: What can be done with the topic? What is its usefulness?
6. Arguing: What can you say for or against your topic?

This exercise can be frustrating to some writers because it requires creative thinking. But at the end of the exercise, it should be obvious what is known or not known about the topic.

Specific Prompting for Specific Writing Assignments

If we want students to write with both power and truth, assisting them in collecting ideas will drastically improve the product. These three writings are designed to help students reflect on and describe themselves. In an

English classroom, these writings are collection devices prior to writing a Personal Statement or college essay, but they also form a platform from which to gauge their own judgment of the characters, settings, and conflicts they will read in a literature classroom.

Mark Edmundson of the University of Virginia argues that the basis of a humanities course is to help the student discover, uncover, and develop their own values and philosophy (2004). Beginning a course by considering an individual stance helps students adjust their position as they journey through the worlds, biases, and views of the content. Writing is the tool to describe rather than prescribe a philosophy. An additional think-write around philosophical questions appears in Appendix C.

The writing-as-product is not the focus of these activities. Rather, the focus is on gathering very individual traits and identity factors. Collecting the insights helps students learn more about themselves. In a course for senior English students the collections will lead to a Personal Statement. The Daybook is a place to hold these "madman" writings before developing the more formal essay. The Personal Statement assignment appears in Appendix C.

Activity #1: The Great Experience

Use this prompt to generate thoughts around student skills: *Write about a time when you did something that you were proud to have accomplished. What was it? What did you do?*

At the beginning of a year this prompt helps students identify skills and talents they already possess. Students in any content can use the activity to describe their strengths to a teacher. When using this with students, I stress that the experience does not need to be school related. Then I model my own *Great Experience*, a time when I managed to get my whole family on a hike—not an easy task when you have college students at home for the summer. This non-work, non-school event emphasizes that the *only* criterion is that the student feels a *great sense of accomplishment*. Before students write, I model my story for the entire class.

After writing, I hand out the Strengths and Skills Checklist (see Appendix C) and model how to use the sheet by asking students to identify my skills and strengths based on the story I have told them. As students tell me what strengths I have, I write the list on the board. Students then pair up and share their experiences with one another. The listener in the partnership uses the list of employment-related skills and strengths to tell the narrator what skills they possess. Even though students use a great experience that comes from their personal lives, they identify strengths and skills that will transfer into the working world.

The list of skills is the goal, reached through the open, self-explorative prompt. Identifying innate strengths in any student will make them more aware of what they can return to for reliable solutions. The sheet has also made the language of the workplace available while showing students that, even if they have not yet been paid for work, they do have experiences they can draw on to do many valuable tasks.

Activity #2: The Ideal Day

Prompt students with these questions and directions: *If you could be paid to do anything, what would that be? Describe the ideal job and your role in that work. If you cannot think of an ideal job, describe the ideal working day. What would you wear? Where and with whom would you work? What kind of tasks would you perform?*

Just as with the *Great Experience*, I model my *Ideal Day* before students write theirs in the ten minutes provided. Afterward I have students identify values for me before I ask them to do this on their own. My list of values is the product of the thinking in writing rather than the writing itself.

This visualization helps students identify what they value. Exploring the ideal day helps students examine and prioritize what is important to them. Again, students will share this writing with a partner and the partner will help them identify a list of values. For instance, if a student spends time describing apparel, the listening student would identify *personal appearance* as a value.

Students need to hear an example first and have a list of what we mean by "values" before exploring this on their own.

Activity #3: People We Admire

Before confronting challenging experiences, we should think about the type of life we imagine for ourselves. Prompt students for this thinking with these directions: *Take about three minutes to list ten people you admire.* (Pause for writing.) *Then, after listing, list the qualities you admire that these people have in common.* After students have written these qualities, point out to them that this is a list of qualities they strive to develop for themselves.

Again, this is a self-discovery writing that helps students identify the qualities. Like the skills and talents writing, students are identifying areas of strength as well as models for how they perceive and judge the world. The list of qualities that results are the qualities they hope to engender in themselves. By moving the assignment to viewing someone outside of themselves, like the character in a book, students now have their own high standards to use for comparison.

In my classes I used these discovery writings prior to assigning a Personal Statement (see Appendix C). This business writing is applicable to students who are entering the workforce or college after their K–12 schooling has ended or as a transitional writing before moving on to high school from middle school.

Collecting for Narratives

It is sometimes hard to walk the line between covering curriculum dictates and centering instruction around student choice. How do we keep students focused on a required product while letting them locate a topic they can adequately explore? A tool I have found eminently flexible comes from Nancie Atwell's *Lessons That Change Writers*. At some point early in any course, I hand them the sheet *Questions for Memoirists*. My seniors have found this tool to be extremely helpful in crafting their college essays. It is clear from the recent changes to the Common Application questions that admissions counselors want a very personal story from their incoming freshmen so they can get an accurate, specific picture of who these students are. The college essay prompts are in Appendix C.

Activity #1: Questions for Memoirists
This is a list of question prompts. Students glue this into the Daybook and are directed to use it whenever they are looking for an idea. The directions are to read through the questions, and when one makes you want to write, you go for it and write. I have personally used the list numerous times and have always found something to write about.

Questions to Get You Started on Some Writing

◆ What are my earliest memories? How far back can I remember?
◆ What are the most important things that have happened to me in my life so far?

- What have I seen that I can't forget?
- What's an incident that shows what my family and I are like?
- What's an incident that shows what my pet(s) and I are like?
- What's something that happened to me at school that I'll always remember?
- What's something that happened to me at home that I'll always remember?
- What's a time when I had a feeling that surprised me?
- What's an incident that changed my life?
- What's a time or place that I was perfectly happy?
- What's a time or place that I laughed a lot?
- What's a time or place when it felt as if my heart were breaking?
- What's a time with a parent that I'll never forget?
- What's a time with a brother or sister that I'll never forget?
- What's a time with a cousin or another relative that I'll never forget?
- Can I remember a time I learned to do something, or did something for the first time?
- What memories emerge when I make a time line of my life so far and note the most important things that happened to me each year?

Once you have the question model, adapt it to your content. I have used this model to write question prompts for teachers who want to write about their profession. Rewrite the questions to prompt thinking in other curricular areas and open student writing to choice.

Here I have adapted Nancie Atwell's Questions for Memoirists to help teachers locate a professional topic for writing.

Review the list of questions below to spur your thinking about practice, and then choose one that makes you want to write:

- What is a classroom event that changed my teaching approach? What happened?
- What is a classroom incident I learned from? What did you learn? How has it changed your teaching?
- Which lesson has proven itself to be a success time and again? What did I do? How do the students gain from it?
- What is a time in teaching that I will never forget?
- What is a teaching "failure" that I have experienced? What did I learn from the experience?

- ◆ What is a teaching "high point" that I remember with fondness? Give it context: What was I doing? What was my goal? What decisions did I make? Why do I consider it a success?
- ◆ What is a teaching situation that made me angry?
- ◆ What philosophy do I hold in my mind as I make decisions in the classroom? Can I think of a time when this worked? Tell a story.
- ◆ Why do I teach?
- ◆ Who has had influence over my teaching career? How does this influence manifest itself in my work?
- ◆ How has education policy shown up in my classroom? Tell a story.

An additional list of journaling questions appears in Appendix A. Since my students will be writing at home on their own as a part of the daily writing exercise, I offer this list to them as a reference when they are stuck for an idea to write about. They glue this list and the *Questions for Memoirists* in their Daybook.

Activity #2: Creating Characters Using Lois Lowry's Method

Most narratives are driven by strong characters. Students can find a way into a story by locating their character first.

Direct students to combine the name of a pet with their street name. Have them try several options until they find one that *makes them want to write*. They can switch out nearby street names or the names of cousins or neighbors until they happen on a name which conjures up strong images. For instance, I have a dog named Oscar and we live near Van Couver Street. My character becomes Oscar Van Couver.

The name prompts the next exploratory writing. *What does the character look like? How old is she/he? What does she/he wear? What job? What are favorite habits, foods, haunts?*

Earnest Hemingway claimed that authors should know far more about their characters than appears in the story. He likened this knowledge to an iceberg. Though a reader will only see the tip of the iceberg, the author must understand the character to the depth and breadth of the much larger submerged portion of the iceberg. This exploratory writing helps the student understand her character.

The next step in the creative narrative is to ask students to develop a conflict. *What problem is the character facing?* If the student has a clear understanding of character, the choices made to resolve the conflict will be much clearer, as will the character's dialogue and descriptions.

Indexing Ideas Within the Daybook Format

After doing any writing for collecting, be sure to show students how to use the index page reserved at the back of the notebook. Students should make an entry on that page (i.e. *Hamlet* character sketch) and then record the page numbers where they have made some preliminary entries. Model how students can keep track of all the thinking and writing they are producing.

More Support for Students: Clean Up Drafts Before Final Assessment

Just prior to handing in major processed papers, I interrupt the process by giving students a class period to review their work one last time, looking for final edits. There is nothing worse than taking home a pile of papers, spending a weekend marking them up only to have students ignore the marks, repeat the mistakes, and learn nothing in the process.

The next time a major paper is due, and MLA formatting (or any required format) and other requirements are a part of your expectations, build in a day for *speed-dating* the paper (Figure 7.1). I generally do this activity on the announced due date. Students arrive with their final draft, only to find that we are going to look at it one more time. I learned the process as *clocking* a paper—sitting in a circle and having students move around the clock face with twelve different stations. My students quickly renamed it *speed-dating*, which I now prefer.

The concept is simple: Half the class acts as an expert on one area of the paper; the other half comprises the moving *daters*. Each student has two minutes to visit an expert, hand over their paper, and have the student close read for specific areas (i.e. *Can the student find and highlight a thesis? Is there specific evidence in each paragraph? Is the paper formatted correctly?* and so forth). Each of the lessons taught in the process of developing the paper should have a student checker. In advance, I make up a 3x5 card with instructions for the checker so they are clear on how to check the paper against expectations. Add in your own pet peeves—those items you are continually correcting.

Daters move on until everyone has visited each station. Then, switch roles and have your checkers become daters.

Every student will leave the class with a draft that needs revising and editing. Then, reset the due date for the final and require that students turn in both the clean draft and the speed-dated draft. Emphasize that students are responsible for making the changes. When I find an outstanding error,

Figure 7.1 Speed-dating the research paper.

I flip back to see if the marked draft included this correction. Usually it has been marked. The student is marked down for not including the correction in the final.

I love taking the time in class for this final check. I receive papers that are more pleasurable to read. All students become experts in at least one area of the paper, while every student gets the message that they are responsible for bringing drafts to a publishable level and that doing so is a complex process requiring multiple readings of the writing. It also reinforces that writing is a social act, sometimes involving many players. Professional writers are subject to the review of editors too, and our students can benefit from this last authentic experience in editing writing.

Bringing students in on a day of editing will help them understand how to control the many rules governing academic writing. Returning this task to students relieves the teacher from the role of copy editor.

Part of our role as teacher is to give our students time to discover their own processes for gathering, formulating, and clarifying thinking in any subject area. English teachers cannot be the sole purveyor of supporting composition. Students need to see how ideas are developed and expressed in every discipline. Reserve some time in your lesson plans to help students discover their own questions and their own voice around the concepts you are teaching. Assignments are opportunities to practice ways of knowing and learning repeatable practices. We can interrupt the process to support student understanding about how to construct a complex final product.

Summing Up

All students need to see how writing is composed in every classroom. We can support this understanding, but it means planning in some writing opportunities long before assignments are due. Short, ungraded writings assist students in finding topics and collecting information they can write about with more clarity. Sharing with peers can help them locate holes in their research or their logic. Finally, letting students do the editing hands over the responsibility for the "rules" while relieving the instructor from many hours of marking papers.

For the Daybook, Incorporate the Following:

◆ Build in opportunities for students to create "hunches" and questions around topics, and encourage students to write freely.
◆ Offer the chance to completely prewrite a paper in a limited amount of time.
◆ Give students real and imagined audiences for their writing. Address early drafts "to a friend" or other person so the ideas flow in the student's own voice.
◆ Let students take on the role of editor and learn from the process. Relieve yourself from the editor's job—a time-consuming and wasted effort.

The next chapter addresses when and how to assess any of the Daybook, madman writings.

8

What About Grading?

Assessing Daily Writing for Growth That Makes the Invisible Visible

"Education is what remains after one has forgotten what one has learned in school."

—Albert Einstein

What to Expect

Inevitably, all teachers must grade the efforts of their students. But if students are writing every day, how much assessment is possible, and when should it occur? If all students in every class are writing, how can the teacher be expected to manage this impossible paper load? This chapter reviews the role of grading as both a motivator for and a detractor from learning. Methods are described to limit grading and to make the evaluation of daily writing one that includes the students, to the benefit of both the student and the instructor.

Chapter Topics

- ◆ Reviewing grading and its effect on student motivation.
- ◆ Creating a low-risk climate for student trial and error.
- ◆ Assessing in real time without formal scoring.
- ◆ Bringing students in on the evaluation.
- ◆ Using writing to assess what students actually learned in an entire course.

A Long History of Carrots and Sticks

Our students have been well conditioned to expect reward for their work. And the reward students expect generally comes in the form of points or grades assigned for nearly every act of performance. Regardless of whether we feel this is a valid expectation, we are all familiar with even the best students demanding *something* for every action in a school setting. The message that all schoolwork must count is well ingrained.

Unfortunately, the assigning of these grades often gets in the way of real learning. Face it: as we gain knowledge and skills, mistakes are going to be made. If every attempt is graded and then averaged together, that grade only reflects the average of our attempts over time rather than the sum of all the attempts and stabs at learning, which we hope would result in real progress.

Oddly, our highest-achieving students, at least according to the gradebook, are adept at producing work for "something" and have grown to expect the highest grades for mere compliance with assigned work. For the most part, these students are avoiding risks that might result in errors. They play it safe for the grade and miss out on an opportunity for real learning.

For students who feel victimized by the mistakes they have made in the past, the construct of grading is very threatening and can result in avoidance tactics. By the time students reach secondary school, both the strugglers and the overachievers are well attuned to both the carrots and sticks of schooling. Our most difficult to teach are most familiar with sticks in the form of zeroes, low grades, and other embarrassments. To save face, many of our students adopt an apathetic pose. If it *doesn't matter* to them, then the slings and arrows have no effect.

Changing the hearts and minds of at-risk students can feel like an uphill battle. Those who have given up on gaining acceptance in the world of school are immune to more zeroes. Even if they squeak by with grades that are barely above failure, it is likely that they are not progressing in their learning at all. Those who have excelled at the compliance model show success grade-wise but little joy or creativity. They are hoop-jumping because the game of schooling is clear.

We have done both groups a disservice. Studies indicate that student interest in school begins to decline in the upper elementary grades and reaches its lowest point in high school. As students separate from schooling goals, dropouts rise (Fredericks and McClosky 2011). The negative effects of grading have a part in this, removing the natural, intrinsic desire to learn and replacing it with an extrinsic one.

The work of William Purkey and Michael Novak explored the conditions for bringing out the human potential in all of us. They coalesced their findings into their *Invitational Theory* (2015). The theoretical assumptions include characteristics which are supported in the exercises outlined in the previous chapters completed in a climate of trust and sharing. Much of what has been suggested in this text—sharing writing, celebrating success, finding prompts which are interesting and focused on student experience—support the theoretical underpinnings of *Invitational Theory*. It has been my experience that our students will flourish under these conditions.

Purkey and Novak claim that bringing about human success requires that we create conditions where it is apparent "that all people matter and can grow through participation in self-governance" (2015, p. 2). They further maintain that our students are ruled by their perception of events (built by reflection) and by the driving question of *Who am I, and how do I fit in the world?* (to develop self-image and efficacy). To bring about these favorable learning conditions references to, we must invite our students into taking risks in their learning within a climate that fosters trust. We must show that we care about individuals and exhibit both our respect for their attempts and the optimism that they can achieve. Many of these claims have been supported in recent educational literature—Dweck's *Mindset* (2006) and the current emphasis on building classroom relationships come to mind.

Into this climate enter grades, which are systematically damaging to the student—both the high achiever and the struggler, as noted above. Grades are the reduction of student achievement to a single descriptor and are ultimately dehumanizing. To counter this in a world where grades are currently required in our roles as educators, I would suggest two things: delay grading for as long as possible so that learning drives the work, and bring students in on the evaluation whenever possible so discussions of quality and achievement—and how to get there—are not a secret.

Overcoming the Grading Conundrum

The easiest way to end the "What kind of grade will I get?" discussion is to make any activity immediately meaningful to the student. As students begin to see a purpose in the method, they will join in. The process of thinking in writing and sharing becomes intrinsically rewarding, not the grade. For at-risk students, repeated exposure to a classroom practice that says, "Trust me, I am not going to hold you responsible for every mistake," will slowly return to our hoped-for role: learner.

Peter Elbow ("Benefits" 1997) maintains that teachers should focus on low-risk, high-frequency writing. Students need lots of practice to improve, but the sting of threat must be removed whenever possible—low-risk. In Chapter 2, it was emphasized that a student's Daybook is their haven for "madman" writing, and that the writing should serve the student. Keeping students writing while maintaining the safe trial and error of written products can be encouraged through two practices: student sharing and student self-evaluation.

Student Sharing as Formative Assessment

Tying writing into your curricular goals will lead to an immediate application of the product. Immediate use can take the form of sharing with a peer; socratic seminars and discussions which reflect the student's written thought; prewrites for longer, assigned papers; and student-as-author sharing in the classroom. These activities are immediately rewarding—whether through the tacit approval of peers or as a satisfying opportunity to learn from each other. The write-then-share construct gives immediate validity to the writing. Sharing provides each student with a window into how a peer conceptualizes or transforms ideas. Students can then "harvest" intellectual reasoning or other student interpretations of content. If you are bolstering this practice through welcoming remarks, honestly noting what a student is doing well, a climate of trust will build with and among the students. You will be modeling acceptance of a variety of voices, and the students will follow your lead.

If student interaction is a goal for the writing, questions about whether the teacher is grading the work quickly dissipate. The reason and purpose behind writing becomes clear—*We are going to have something to share, and I will be successful because I have something to share*. Students also receive an immediate reward: someone is listening to their ideas and responding with interest or enthusiasm.

When writing is assigned that is intended as a collection for assignments and lets students explore their thinking around a topic, or they are searching for the important nuggets in a reading, all completed for curricular goals, then an immediate use for the writing becomes self-evident and grades become beside the point.

A second strength to student sharing lies in the fact that the writer reads his or her own writing. There are several advantages here for the at-risk student. First, no one sees the writing but the writer. The surface errors that color both teacher and peer perception of at-risk-students as inferior are invisible, and student thought rises to center stage. This is a level of safety that most at-risk students do not enjoy. Secondly, the writer begins to hear his or her own written voice and to discover they *do* have thoughts connected with content. This has great power in shaping the student's self-image as a maker of meaning. Finally, the sharing allows all writers to evaluate themselves in relation to their peer group rather than in relation to the master reader and writer in the classroom: the teacher. For an at-risk student, this begins to build a model of the possible. In other words, sharing student work helps the struggling student see possibilities within the assignment that are accessible because they have been produced and modeled by peers. Sharing in a positive *Let's see what you are doing right* community acknowledges Purkey and Novak's condition that all humans are able, valuable, and responsible.

 Teacher Tip

When students share, genuinely listen for something to praise—even if it is only the courage to go public. Naming student strengths (*You're a poet/historian/thinker*) will drive self-image in new directions. More than one student has risen to the expectations implied in the new identity.

In terms of evaluation of student work by the teacher, hearing student thought daily is ideal formative assessment. Through discussion, teachers can provide early correction of misunderstanding; that is, if a peer hasn't already made the adjustment for the teacher—which is the best possible outcome. Finding consensus in group sharing and discussion ultimately arrives at the essential content of a course. Additionally, both divergent and convergent ideas will surface, rather than limiting classroom interaction to only one read on the topic: a teacher's. These insights can take the class far beyond the curricular expectations and are a bonus. When the divergent idea comes from those previously seen as at-risk or outside our construct of the ideal student, the rewards are life altering.

Back in the Real World

Grading can limit student achievement. In the Advanced Placement course, Todd, an athlete and able student who initially confessed to writing only to achieve the minimum to meet grade expectations, declared himself a poet after experimenting with the genre in daily writing activities tied to our unit on poetry.

The largely ungraded Daybook offers the opportunity to experiment with "writerly moves" while simultaneously evaluating written works. The practice is beneficial to learning writer's craft, but often results in changing students' perceptions of themselves as writers. Having been given the safe, ungraded space to experiment, Todd began to see value in writing as a tool of self-expression. His pieces reflected his enthusiasm and joy in sport. In his own words, he was "proud" of the poetry he produced and "surprised" to find he liked it, a genre he had shown no interest in before. A straight-A student, he had been unwilling to take any risks with an elusive genre that might endanger his carefully groomed grade point average. The Daybook provided the space to "cut loose" without risking a grade. For our most compliant students, those who will not risk mistakes as they strive for top honors, this is probably the greatest gift we can give them—encouragement to play, experiment, and assess their own efforts without our interference.

Student Self-Assessment Through Audits for Formative and Summative Assessment

The kids are writing daily, they are engaged in their thinking, and generating lots and lots of written work. In addition, you are serving over 100 students. This begs the question: "Do I have to read it all?" Daily writing times a hundred, after all, is much, much more writing than a teacher can physically handle.

How you handle your part of the bargain depends, as most good teaching does, on what students need as motivation to maintain their practice. Remember, students gain skills from regular practice, and the primary goal is facilitating practice. Grading has the effect of ending practice. Save this task for as late in the process as possible.

The objective in assessing the kinds of writing done in a Daybook should focus on this question: *Are they doing the exercises? Can they identify their own process and growth? Are they generating the amount of writing and thinking that moves skill forward or accesses the curricular goals?*

If compliance with exercises is one of the goals, the students themselves can easily handle that assessment for you.

Early in your new writing practice it is helpful to work with the Daybook daily—at least for the first twenty-one days—the magic number that some have said is necessary to form a new habit. Even if twenty-one days is arbitrary, the repeated classroom routine will set the tone for your expectations. At that point, a quick assessment on whether students are keeping up with the new practice can be completed in class—this would enhance the usual casual observance of student activity up to this point. It will also confirm for those students who need it that participation does matter.

Ask students to "audit" their books and then turn in both the Daybook and the audit. If the audit is done at the beginning of class, you can assess each class quickly before students leave while they are engaged in other practice work. At this stage, you need only count their entries. Returning the books to them before they leave reinforces the idea that the writing is their personal property and is a safe place to try, and possibly fail, as they learn a new skill. The teacher assessment of the audit merely confirms that the student self-assessment is validated by the Daybook. When students know you will be looking at their assessment, you generally get honest student evaluation.

By turning the task over to the students, you bring them in on evaluation. In addition, your questions on the audit serve to review and reinforce expectations. This early audit will help students adjust their work to meet expectations and find success later. It will also give you the opportunity to pull students aside for a short conference. Consider the following as a model: "I noticed you are not keeping up with the writing. How can I help you?"

Here is an example of a simple audit. Adapt this idea to your own personal objectives for the informal writing. A sample early audit appears in Chapter 2.

Provide students with a half sheet of paper. Ask students to do three things:

- ◆ **Count their entries**. Remember, every entry should be dated. This makes the entries easy to find. If students have not been doing this, they will see the usefulness of the practice as they review their work.
- ◆ **Count the words per entry and provide an average word count**. This is a chance for students to see how much language they are generating.
- ◆ **Ask students to compare an early entry to a later one**. What are they noticing? Can they describe what they see themselves doing in the notebook?
- ◆ **Have students set a new goal**. A simple question can be included in the audit to challenge students to improve. Try: *What will you do to reinforce this new habit?*

Remember the assumption of *Invitational Theory*—people will take responsibility if you expect it of them. Ask students to develop solutions to the problem of practice. When we take the responsibility, and that includes meting out punishments for non-compliance, we are indicating that they are incapable of shaping their own destiny and do not learn to *self*-discipline.

When reviewing the books, focus on the student-completed audit. Quickly peruse the book to confirm the student entry count. It may not even be necessary to count entries if it looks as though the student has come close enough to their own count. At this point you may either provide feedback in the form of points that reflect the student engagement or in the form of praise and a focusing question. Either way, this activity should be deemphasized as a grade. It is best to use it as a starting point that students can refer to later to evaluate how they are adapting, using, and growing in their writing practices.

End-of-Unit Assessment

If students have been using the Daybook to think in writing about your curriculum, ask students to produce writing from the daily writings that shows their understanding. This would mean looking at only one or two entries rather than the entire book.

Bob Tierney, a former biology teacher, asked his struggling students to keep their notebooks in the room. Part of this decision stemmed from the students' need for help with organization and, from time to time, he would ask them to open the notebook to the page where they "explained photosynthesis" or another concept. The students left the notebooks in the class bin opened to the page they had located which represented their learning around the topic. At the end of the day, Tierney would flip through the bins, reading the students thoughts and then marking them with a check or whatever feedback the student needed. There is no better window into a student's understanding than by reading their thoughts, and he gained insight into how well students were understanding the content.

Tierney argued repeatedly that all teachers are the "Emperor of Points" and as such can give students whatever they demand if it keeps kids moving forward. Another technique Tierney used was stamping the word *Zorch!* at random on student work. Though the word carried no weight, students were invariably pleased when they found *Zorch!* stamped at the top. Sometimes all we crave is a little validation.

I began the practice of marking *sparkly thoughts* in student logs with a hand-drawn star. I learned this simple and quick feedback tool from veteran North Carolina English teacher Dixie Dellinger. It is a quick and simple response that notes where students are shining in their thinking. Later, this practice is transferred to the students. When they share response logs, students are reminded to tell their partners when they hear a *sparkly thought*, an opportunity for students to listen for insightful comments, unique perspectives, or deep thinking. The student then marks his or her own draft with a star. In this way, each student is a partner in evaluation that rewards good work. Students love to look through their writing to find a *sparkly thought* from me or receive affirmation from their peers. Though the stars carry no grading weight, they are much prized—even more than As.

I can't help but notice how grading seems to devalue the work our students are doing. In the poetry unit, we wrote poems daily yet none of them were graded. From this regular practice, many students proclaimed themselves converts to the genre. This should be telling us once again to reserve summative grades for as long as is humanly possible.

Assessing the Daybook

My students perform two audits of their Daybook in my course. The first is the twenty-one-day are-you-forming-the-habit? assessment. The second takes place midway through the course. On this day, I always plan a quiet activity so I can assess their Daybooks in front of them and return the books to them before they leave. Most of the time I can get through all the books before they leave. For those I don't, I tell them the book will be done by the end of the day so they can come by and pick it up. Most of them do. That is a tacit indication of the value they place on their writing.

In this second audit, I ask them to review their entire book looking for patterns. The evaluation is primarily so they can begin to note their own habits and rituals. Then they are asked to mark two of the entries. One is for "Original Thought" and the other is a writing they deem of "High Quality." Both are goals for the activity and the course. My job is to read and respond to the audit, count entries, and then read and respond to the two entries they mark as meeting the criteria established. My feedback on the two entries is generally a reader response, not an evaluator's. All my responses appear on the audit, and I do not mark in the Daybooks.

 Teacher Tip

Respond to writing as a reader first. Distinguishing between responding as an evaluator and as a reader is important. How does an evaluator respond? That person assigns a quality to the writing: good, boring, slow, needs detail, etc. A reader responds to content: "Oh, you lost your dog? I'm so sorry. That must have been heart wrenching." Teachers should respond to the ideas of the writing first, before asking questions that might move the writing forward.

When students share their inner thoughts in a risk-free space, they are not looking to be judged. They want to be heard. To keep students writing and thinking we must validate their thoughts, show interest, curiosity, empathy. So, respond as an interested reader. Confirm the message rather than assigning scores to their thoughts.

Finally, I do assign a score to this mid-course audit (Figure 8.1). It is a flat point score which we have negotiated as a class. During the Daybook activities, I have kept a desk calendar marking the days when we have used the Daybook in class. For my composition course, the students are also assigned daily writing outside of class, hoping to help them form a habit of building fluency by routinely transferring thought to writing. Each student should make an entry for each day on the calendar in addition to the writing we have done together in class. In this way, I hope to have students find topics, methods, habits of mind while shedding a fear of getting perfect writing down on paper. If you must write *something* daily, surely some of it will be drivel, so who cares? Just write.

Figure 8.1 Daybook audit example.

Daybook Audit

The goal of writing in the Daybook is to develop fluency (following your thoughts in writing) through daily writing about topics of interest to you. Our goal was to have an entry every day. No matter how close you came to this goal, take some time now to review your writing:

How many entries do you have to date? _____
What is the average length of an entry (word count)? _____

Complete this exercise described by Natalie Goldberg in *Writing Down the Bones*:

Sit down and reread your whole Daybook as if it isn't yours. "Become curious: 'What did this person have to say?' Make yourself comfortable and settle down as though it were a good novel you were about to read. Read it page by page. Even if it seemed dull when you wrote it, now you will recognize its texture and rhythm."

Then, reflect in the space below about what you see. Note where you could have pushed further and out of laziness or avoidance didn't. See where you are truly boring, or how complaining just leads to a deeper pit. Comment: who do you seem to be in this book?

Read your Mission Statement on the first page. Comment on how you planned to use your Daybook and how that plan has developed. What kind of commitment have you made to the process?

Which kind of entry did you find easiest to accomplish?

Are there any recurring themes in your Daybook? Are there issues that repeatedly surface?

What did you notice about the process? What have you gained from thinking daily in writing?

A goal of daily writing is to increase fluency—that is, to be able to move thoughts more quickly from the mind to the paper. Comment on your own fluency below:

Mark two of your entries. Flag one that you feel is an example of original thinking (your ideas, not borrowed ideas). Label it: *Original.* Flag another one that you feel reveals qualities of good writing. Label it: *High Quality.* Below list the reasons you feel each entry qualifies as original or reflects good quality.

Finally, turn the Daybook in to me with this sheet. I will COUNT ENTRIES ONLY. I will look only at the entries you have marked as *Original Thought* and *High Quality.*

About a week before the Daybook is audited I let the class know how many entries they would have if they had been completely faithful to the process. The number might be as high as eighty-five entries. Then we negotiate. Since few of us are perfect, I ask the students what number out of eighty-five would they consider an "A" effort. Whatever the class decides becomes the number of points awarded. For instance, seventy points would be 100%.

Many students far exceed the agreed upon number because they have seen the assignment as opportunity to meet one of their own goals. Others flounder. But now they know their own grade. If they want to improve it before the due date, all they must do is write. And writing, for a composition course, is a chief goal.

Figure 8.1 is an example of a recent audit. I adjust the questions each term to reflect our practice and my current curiosity about their work.

Writing Prior to Other Assessment

Purposeful and personally relevant writing that serves student learning should be a primary lesson for all curricula. Probably the cleverest method for driving this point home is pre-assessment writing that overtly does exactly that: serve student learning while revealing the power of personal note making.

Activity #1: 3x5 Study Guide

Prior to a major unit assessment, provide every student with a 3x5 card. Tell them they can bring the card to the testing setting and may include anything on the card that they wish to use as a guide.

For students who never study or review notes, the 3x5 card promise will ensure that those students do just that: review notes, reread, and make notes that are meaningful to them to use as a "crib" on the test—provided all those notes fit in the confines of the 3x5 card.

What must a student do to fulfill the promise of the notecard? This activity involves many intellectual moves on the part of the student. Some may try to cram all the details into small print, and thus will review all the material in the process. Others may look for large, essential ideas from the content to include on the card. This activity requires a sifting and sorting by the student to winnow information down to the large ideas. Others may only put ideas on the card that they struggle with throughout the unit. Still others will list vocabulary that is endemic to the content.

In every case the student will be differentiating learning and identifying areas of individual concern and struggle. Finally, the act of writing the concepts on the card will filter the information through their own language and cement the concepts.

Many students find that, after reviewing and writing down information from the unit, they do not need much or any of the information from the card. In addition to learning the material, the student has learned a process for digesting the material—reviewing and note making (not note copying).

Activity #2: Daybook Quizzes

If you want assurance that students are completing in-class Daybook activities or you want to inspire more careful thinking and writing, you can give students a Daybook Quiz. Simply design a short quiz in which they must locate answers in the Daybook and quote passages on the quiz. This eliminates the need to collect and lug all those journals around.

Final Assessment of Learning—End-Of-Course Portfolio or Demonstrated Learning

As was mentioned at the beginning of the chapter, we have dug ourselves into a hole with students by grading everything to ensure compliance and by averaging all the student attempts at learning. The averaging of grades is not a reflection of what the student learned. Ideally, at the end of the course it should be clear to everyone what the objectives were and how students are performing in relation to those objectives.

Learning is a very individual process and students will learn at different rates based on their prior knowledge, how hard they work, and their level of interest. The end-of-course portfolio becomes a document where the student must account for his or her own learning.

In a writing classroom, there will be many artifacts that speak to students' engagement with the course material, and collecting and reflecting on those artifacts will chart student progress through a course.

Prior to the end of the course, students are directed to search through their notebooks and collected writing to find examples of where they gained an understanding of curricular concepts. These become the artifacts that confirm their learning and the process. Teachers can direct students to annotate the selected works by explaining why they have chosen the piece of evidence and what learning it exemplifies.

There are several ways to approach the Portfolio, but every method ensures that the student must reflect on an entire body of course work and select examples of where they mastered a concept or finally had a break-through moment.

In a composition class, my students must present the entire body of work in a Portfolio (see Chapter 4 on reflection) and can view their work over time. The reflective writings indicate the gains they can support in their own process. The complete Portfolio assignment appears in Appendix B. Content area teachers will want students to assemble evidence of the attainment of essential understandings.

Teachers who implement Portfolios in their classroom may want to include a requirement that the Daybook, as a central learning tool in the classroom, be addressed as a part of the Portfolio.

For the assessment piece of daily writing, knowledge of your students and their needs should guide when and how grades are managed. It is also helpful to understand the conditions surrounding the writing. This includes knowing who you expect your student to be writing for (self, peer, an examiner). I have used the *Sense of Audience* categories (Figure 8.2) to determine where my response to the writing falls. Knowing

Figure 8.2 Sense of audience categories.

SENSE OF AUDIENCE CATEGORIES
(use to determine instructor response)

Child (or adolescent) to self
Requires only that it is complete.
Many of the prompted daily writings fall in this category.
Can be adjusted, added to, changed to match student need.

Child (or adolescent) to trusted adult
Provides a caring, reader's response focused on ideas.
This can include teachers and parents. Provide feedback, not a grade.

Pupil to teacher as partner in dialogue
This is formative assessment, where teachers can note successes
and ask questions that move student learning forward. No grade required, just feedback.

Pupil to teacher seen as examiner or assessor
The teacher's role shifts from helper to examiner. If students are brought in on
forming requirements and assessing and adjusting along the way,
a final assessment should not be a shock.

Writer to his readers (or his public)
These writings go beyond the classroom and are both
highly motivating and have the potential to realize
the most gains in learning. The "assessment" comes from
reader feedback and response. No grade, just celebrating.

Increased risk for the writer.

the intended audience for the exercise helps me determine how the piece will be assessed. Be sure to bring your students in on this thinking so they understand the variable purposes of writing as well. Sometimes the writer is the only one who needs to see the writing (note making, collecting, brainstorming). At other times, there will be an outside audience that supports or coaches. Risk of exposure on the part of the writer increases as the level of audience rises.

When we better understand who our students are writing for and why, we can assess the writing in a manner that is consistent with our goals.

Though assessment is often last on our minds, developing a culture of learning should drive every decision made about when and how to grade student work and is worth our first thoughts as we develop assignments and graded evaluations.

For our struggling students, the punitive nature of grades is often the enemy to growth. For students who excel at schooling (as opposed to learning), grading is also a limiter to growth. We need to arrange our classrooms to ensure a high opportunity for success. The Daybook is the safe space for practice, and treating it as such will benefit every student in the room. But that safety can extend to the entire course and the classroom itself. Ensuring success may mean leaving the tools for daily writing (pens, pencils, notebooks) in the room for easy access. It means finding moments to celebrate while delaying grades until students can work their way to a satisfactory level of mastery.

It also means continually exhibiting care and respect for student ideas and creating a climate of trust and optimism that helps everyone realize their human potential.

Summing Up

Grading has the potential to damage the innate desire to learn. When we use grades to motivate, students quickly grow disaffected with learning and shift their focus to hanging onto points rather than taking a risk and surprising themselves. Delaying or deemphasizing grading can free students to explore, while simultaneously freeing teachers from marking every scrap of paper. If we bring students in on evaluating products, they can describe their own growth and achievements. This assessment goes far beyond a letter grade.

For the Daybook, Incorporate the Following:

◆ Eliminate student questions about grades and points by providing an immediate use for writing.

◆ Ask students to locate writing which fulfills classroom goals and look only at those.

◆ Know your purpose in assigning the writing. Only use assessment where it matches that purpose.

◆ Ask students to describe their own learning to you. Bringing students in on evaluation is yet another intellectual behavior we can instill in students: examining quality.

Afterword

It is the first day of class. I am nervous, and so are my students. The room is silent, all eyes on me and everyone on their best behavior—cell phones put away, first day outfits and hair neatly in place. I can tell they know what to expect—teacher after teacher will fill the day reviewing expectations, syllabi, class rules—no need to engage the brain as we sleep walk our way through a whole day of blah-blah-blah.

This class feels foreign to me. I am not used to twenty-five teenagers in mute silence. I am talking too much. Where is the chatter?

Even after three decades of working with students, the first day is still nerve wracking. Here is a group of strangers I need to get to know very quickly. Will we be able to make a connection? Will they relate to the *old* woman, *white* woman, just plain *woman*, the intruding adult? We will have to trust each other if we have a hope of getting to the tough stuff. After all, our curriculum involves asking all the big human questions: *Why do we suffer? What is my purpose here if it only ends in death? How do I express my love/hate/suffering/joy to you in a way that helps you see and feel my love/hate/suffering/joy?* If literature and writing are going to come to life, we must lay it all on the line.

But I have an ace in this game. With all the world's knowledge online, in our pockets, and available at the press of a button, I have something the cyber world does not: living, breathing humans all together in one place at the same time. Capitalizing on that dynamic is my goal, and writing is the tool we'll use to pry us open. To get students interacting with and pushing each other in new directions, we must build a community that works together. We must know each other and agree to be helpful and caring. We will start on the first day.

On day one, we write. And then we share. And then we write again. Writing uncovers truths and sharing those builds the face-to-face community I need to get big things done.

My students are grouped at tables—to take the focus off the teacher. I model brief stations along my own reading journey, describing my struggles and successes. Then they write and share theirs. By the end of our hour and a half together, the room is smiling, sharing, chatting, talking about books they loved, hated, want to read again. Finally, they take home pages of notes for the introductory reflective essay they will share with me.

Now I recognize my classroom. We are starting to feel like we belong together.

In the informal reflection assigned that day, students will tell me the story of their lives as readers. I will get to know their favorite childhood books, the books they loved, the books they avoided, the struggles with reading. I will also begin to hear unique voices lifting off the page. Reading at home, it seems as if we are sitting side by side as I listen to their story.

The earliest writings help me know these students as people. The quiet introvert describes a classic reading list longer than mine, the energetic athlete confesses to a hidden hobby of reading non-fiction, the orphaned girl misses the mom who read to her as a toddler, an Advanced Placement student confesses to faking reading until it all came together late one night at the age of ten—in the fifth grade.

These are papers I look forward to reading. As I read, I picture their faces and link the story to a person. Since learning about my students is my goal, I throw away the red pen. My comments are simple. A smiley face in the margins where a tender moment made me smile. A check mark where something is written especially well. A star to mark a *sparkly thought* where the student's thinking pushed my own. I react to their ideas. Sometimes I talk back to the student writing: *Ha, Ha! That's priceless. True that. OMG, what happened? Thanks for sharing.* Always, always, *thanks for sharing.* My reactions are honest, but I am also hoping to send this message: *I am listening.* Writing is about thoughts, feelings, and ideas. I confirm: message received. Everyone needs to know they've been heard. We can work on the other stuff later.

On separate paper, I start taking notes. What do my students already grasp that I can encourage? Where are there gaps we need to address? These notes are for my instruction. There is a list—who might need certain things from me, or who could they get this from in the class? Even those who are excelling can still go to the next step. I write the observations down, but rarely refer to them. My students are now three-dimensional, with weaknesses *and* strengths, with stories, with desires and hopes. They have resources to capitalize on as we go through our readings and writings. Even now, when I encounter the students as adults, I remember those stories and feel the bonds we developed together while they still had that amazing adolescent willingness to take a risk and share, and I was the lucky witness.

There is no better window into the student's mind and heart than through writing. If I need to know something about my teaching or their learning, I need only ask. And then attend to the answer. I will learn something every time.

Thank goodness day one is over.

We are off and running.

Works Cited

Adler, Mortimer J. *The Paideia Proposal: An Educational Manifesto*. Touchstone, 1 October 1998.

Allington, Richard L. and Rachael E. Gabriel. "Every Child, Every Day." *Educational Leadership*, vol. 69, no. 6, 2012, pp. 10–15.

Atwell, Nancie. *Lessons That Change Writers*. Heinemann, 2002. Print.

Blair, Hugh. *Lectures on Rhetoric and Belles Lettres* (Vol. 1). James Decker, 1801. https://books.google.com/books

Blau, Sheridan. *The Literature Workshop: Teaching Texts and Their Readers*. Heinemann, 2003. Print.

Britton, James. "The Composing Process and the Functions of Writing." *Research on Composing: Points of Departure*. Ed. Charles Cooper and Lee Odell. NCTE, 1978, pp. 13–28. Print.

Clark, Roy Peter. *Writing Tools: 50 Essential Strategies for Every Writer*. Little, Brown and Company, 2006. Print.

Currey, Mason. *Daily Rituals*. Knopf, 2013. Print.

Di Stefano, Giada, Francesca Gino, Gary Pisano and Bradley Staats. *Learning by Thinking: How Reflection Aids Performance*. Working Paper: HEC Paris. 25 March 2014. PDF.

Dweck, Carol S. *Mindset: The New Psychology of Success*. Random House, 2006. Print.

Edmundson, Mark. *Why Read?* Bloomsbury, 2004. Print.

Elbow, Peter. "Benefits of Low Stakes Writing (Writing to Learn)." *Assigning and Responding to Writing in the Disciplines*. Ed. Mary Deane Sorcinelli and Peter Elbow Jossey-Bass, 1997. PDF. http://effectivegradingpractices forwriting.wikispaces.com/file/view/benefitsoflowstakeswriting. pdf/529906216/benefitsoflowstakeswriting.pdf

Elbow, Peter. "Grading Student Writing: Making It Simpler, Fairer, Clearer." *New Directions for Teaching and Learning*, vol. 69, 1997, pp. 127–140. PDF.

Elbow, Peter. "High Stakes and Low Stakes in Assigning and Responding to Writing." *New Directions for Teaching and Learning*, vol. 69, 1997, pp. 41–52.

Elbow, Peter. *Writing With Power: Techniques for Mastering the Writing Process*. Oxford University Press, 1998. Print.

Emig, Janet. "Writing as a Mode of Learning." *College Composition and Communication*, vol. 28, no. 2, 1977, pp. 122–128. Print.

"English Language Arts Standards 'Anchor Standards' College and Career Readiness Anchor Standards for Writing 10." *Common Core State Standards Initiative*. Web. 31 July 2014. Online.

Flowers, Betty. "Madman, Architect, Carpenter, Judge: Roles in the Writing Process." *Language Arts*, vol. 58, no. 7, 1981, pp. 834–836. Print.

Fredericks, Jennifer and Wendy McCloskey. *Measuring Student Engagement in Upper Elementary Through High School: A Description of 21 Instruments*. Regional Educational Laboratory Southeast. January 2011. https://ies.ed.gov/ncee/edlabs/regions/southeast/pdf/REL_2011098.pdf

Gallagher, Kelly. *Teaching Adolescent Writers*. Stenhouse, 2006. Print.

Graves, Donald. *Teachers and Children at Work*. Heinemann. 1983. Print.

Heller, Rafael. "The Scope of the Adolescent Literacy Crisis." *All About Adolescent Literacy*. WETA, 2017. www.adlit.org/adlit_101/scope_of_the_adolescent_literacy_crisis/

Karpicke, Jeffry D. and Janell R. Blunt. "Retrieval Practice Produces More Learning Than Elaborative Studying With Concept Mapping." *Science*, 20 January 2011. PDF. www.physics.emory.edu/faculty/weeks//journal/karpicke-sci11a.pdf

Lamott, Anne. *Bird by Bird: Some Instructions on Writing and Life*. Pantheon Books, 1994. Print.

Lederer, Richard. "The Case for Short Words." *The Miracle of Language*. Gallery Books, 1999, pp. 30–33. Print.

Mueller, Pam A. and Daniel M. Oppenhiemer. "The Pen Is Mightier Than the Keyboard." *Psychological Science*, vol. 25, no. 5, 2014, pp. 1159–1168.

The National Commission on Writing. *Writing: A Ticket to Work . . . Or a Ticket Out*. College Board. September 2004. PDF. www.collegeboard.com/prod_downloads/writingcom/writing-ticket-to-work.pdf

Newkirk, Thomas. *The Essential Don Murray*. Heinemann, 2009. Print.

Pirsig, Robert M. *Zen and the Art of Motorcycle Maintenance: An Inquiry Into Values*. Morrow, 1974. Print.

Purkey, William Watson and Joh Michael Novak. *An Introduction to Invitational Theory*. September 2015. PDF. www.invitationaleducation.net/docs/samples/art_intro_to_invitational_theory.pdf

Rosenthal, Amy Krouse. *Encyclopedia of an Ordinary Life*. Crown Publishing Group, 2005. Print.

Simon, Cecelia Capuzzi. "Veterans Learn to Write and Heal." *The New York Times*, February 1, 2013. www.nytimes.com/2013/02/03/education/edlife/veterans-learn-to-write-and-heal.html

U.S. Department of Education. *Writing 2011: National Assessment of Educational Progress at Grades 8 and 12*. National Center for Education

Statistics: Institute of Education Sciences. 2011. PDF. https://nces. ed.gov/nationsreportcard/pdf/main2011/2012470.pdf

Weinstein, Larry. *Writing at the Threshold*. National Council of Teachers of English, 2001. Print.

Willingham, Daniel. "Why Don't Students Like School? Because the Mind Is Not Designed for Thinking." *American Educator*, Spring 2009, pp. 4–13. Print. www.aft.org/sites/default/files/periodicals/WILLINGHAM%282%29.pdf

Wrigley, Robert. "After a Rainstorm." *Poetry Out Loud*. Poetry Foundation and the National Endowment for the Arts, 2016. 21 December 2016. Online. http://www.poetryoutloud.org/poems-and-performance/poems/detail/54867

Appendix A

Additional Prompting

Sources for Additional Prompts

Books

What If? Writing Exercises for Fiction Writers, Third Edition by Anne Bernays and Pamela Painter. Pearson, 2009. Great prompts to help students develop ideas for all aspects of narrative and fictional writing.

What Can I Write About? 7,000 Topics for High School Students, Second Edition by David Powell. NCTE, 2002. No longer in print, you'll have to find this book in a used bookstore or online. Topic ideas are divided into content areas, so this is not just for English teachers.

Writing Down the Bones: Freeing the Writer Within by Natalie Goldberg. Shambhala, 2016. Recently celebrating a thirtieth anniversary edition in 2016, this is the compilation of Goldberg's work in teaching writing through workshops to help new writers find their purpose. Many prompts provided to free that writer.

Writing as a Road to Self-Discovery by Barry Lane. Discover Writing Company, 1998. This is filled with many writing exercises. Lane uses three tools for exploring a life: remembering, reframing, and re-experiencing. These follow the reflecting pattern of: What happened? So what? And now what?

The Book of Questions by Gregory Stock, Ph.D. Workman Publishing, 2013. Many of the questions in this book require the answerer to consider a moral stance before answering. Intended as an adult conversation generator, you will find it necessary to choose questions appropriate for your age group. However, my students have always enjoyed thinking in writing first about their own personal answer to some deeply ethical questions.

Deeper Reading: Comprehending Challenging Texts, 4–12 by Kelly Gallagher. Stenhouse, 2004. Gallagher provides many ways to help students tackle those texts required in both English and the content areas, wherever we have students read and think.

The Literature Workshop: Teaching Texts and Their Readers by Sheridan Blau. Heinemann, 2003. This book is heavy on theory but walks teachers through writing exercises which help students better understand the intellectual work of responding to text and developing papers. My students, in all levels, responded with enthusiasm to the prompting in this book.

Websites

Writing prompts for **social studies and history**. Teachers created these prompts. Some are interesting "what ifs?" Others are prompts from photographs. There are sure to be several that can be tied to a unit of study.

http://writingprompts.tumblr.com/post/30655462866/writing-prompts-for-social-studies-history

650 Prompts for Narrative and Personal Writing. This amazing resource is created by The Learning Network of *The New York Times*. There is also an additional link for debate topics. Every prompt is tied to a news story. All 650 are divided by topic and can be used in many disciplines. (Includes questions on morality, money and social class, technology, gender, history, and many others.) Follow the tinyurl below.

http://tinyurl.com/650prompts

Questions that inspire curiosity and problems to solve can be found at websites that feature news around the subject area. This also brings current issues and new questions about a subject into the classroom.

Here are good sources for think-writes in the subject area:

For math questions: www.scientificamerican.com/math.
For prompting in science: www.nsf.gov/discoveries.
For history: www.hisory.com/news/ask-history or Smithsonian
   Tween Tribune: tweentribune.com.

Join www.najowrimo.org/. This is based on the popular **National Novel in a Month** challenge to write toward a novel during every day in the month of November. This challenge runs through four months of the year—January, April, July, and October—and provides journaling prompts for both the new and the experienced writer. They arrive in the inbox every day of January.

What if? This blog seriously answers absurd questions with scientific and physics reasoning. The questions could be fun think-writes in science classes. Or buy the book *What If? Serious Scientific Answers to Absurd Hypothetical Questions* culled from the website by the blog's author Randall Monroe.

https://what-if.xkcd.com

Apps

A quick search at the App Store reveals that there are many electronic journaling tools. Among them:

Gratitude Journal
Day One
Five Minute Journal

Prompts or affirmations are usually provided.

Question Prompts for Journaling

Directions: Read the list and choose one that makes you want to write. Set a timer for ten minutes and write the entire time. See where your thinking leads. If you have nothing to write, just write, "I have nothing to write."

- How am I feeling right now?
- How old do I feel today and why?
- Why am I trying to write?
- Why do I always _____?
- How can I heal my relationship with _____?
- Why don't I want to see _____?
- What makes me feel successful?
- What makes me feel like a failure?
- Why isn't _____ responding the way I want?
- What is my goal right now?
- What's the best way to achieve my goal?
- What do I want most in my life right now?
- What am I willing to change about myself?
- What is my greatest strength?
- What is my greatest weakness?
- What am I reluctant to share?
- What do I really want to say to _____?
- What turns me on?
- What turns me off?
- What do I really want?
- When am I the happiest?
- What brings tears to my eyes? A lump to my throat?
- Who do I think others see when they look at me?

Appendix B

Reflecting and Goal Setting

Figure A1 About the Author additional assignment for the Daybook.

How do I write an *About the Author* blurb?

Start with your name and where you were born. If you did not grow up where you were born, tell about the other places you grew up.

Write in third person (no "I" or "me" in the text).

Chose a style: serious, literary, humorous, youthful, poetic, or mix and match.

Reveal some of your life experiences, ambitions, family, cultural, or religious background—something that relates to your life interests and the kinds of things about which you would choose to write if it were up to you.

Finally, tell us why you write—what really motivates you to sit down and write.

Now it's your turn. Write your *About the Author* blurb below. Read it to a partner and fix errors before moving it into your Daybook. To make it look professional, bring in a photo to add to the page. Your About the Author blurb should go on the inside back cover. Glue it in.

Notes:	Mary Tedrow
Name Birthplace Background	Mary Tedrow was born in Washington "D.C." and spent most of her childhood in Kensington, Maryland, buying comic books and penny candy so she could read and eat in her favorite crabapple tree.
Nice image	
Shows how background influences writing.	Mary is one of five children and was often found quietly observing the antics of her siblings and the hordes of children who were her neighbors. These experiences still influence the events of her writing today
Occupation/experience Current life situation	She has been teaching high school English since 1978. During that time she has also worked in advertising, news reporting, freelance writing, and as a secretary.
Unexpected/unknown fact	She credits her success with the sometimes rambunctious high school students she teaches to her years serving as a bartender in Front Royal.

© 2018 Mary Tedrow

Initial Self-Assessment

Reading Name: _____

1. I enjoy reading the following types of print:
   ___ books   ___ magazines   ___ newspapers
   ___ poems   ___ short stories   ___ plays

2. I choose to read books that are not assigned in school . . .
   ___ often   ___ sometimes   ___ never

3. My attitude about reading is . . .
   ___ positive   ___ neutral   ___ negative

4. I like to read books from the following genres:
   ___ nonfiction/informational   ___ historical fiction
   ___ traditional fantasy   ___ modern fantasy/low
   ___ modern fantasy/high   ___ non-fiction/biography
   ___ science fiction   ___ non-fiction/autobiography
   ___ realistic fiction/adventure ___ realistic fiction/mystery
   ___ realistic fiction/classics   ___ realistic fiction/humor
                                    ___ romance/relationship stories

5. When I compare books that I have really enjoyed, some things
   they all have in common are: _____

   _____

6. The best book I've ever read is: _____

   _____

7. Some of my favorite authors are: _____

   _____

8. I could improve my reading skills if: _____

   _____

9. People whose book recommendations I value include: _____

   _____

10. I could make more time for recreational reading if: _____

    _____

11. A reading goal that I would like to achieve for this school year
    is: _____

The Benchmark Assignments

We have done a series of activities that I call "benchmark" activities. These were designed to help you assess your abilities upon entering a course of reading, analysis, and composition and then set goals for growth. Please set these assignments aside and refer to them when creating your course goals, discussing your work with your parents at the student-led parent conference, and at the end of the course when you are demonstrating your own growth in the Portfolio.

These are the assignments:

1. Initial Summer Reading Logs and the "Myself as a Reader" reflections.
2. The AP Reading Comprehension test.
3. The "Hawk and Golden Retriever" poetry essay.

After we review each of the benchmark assessments, take a few moments to jot down the areas of strength and areas for potential growth as personal goals for your achievement in this course.

1. Reading Logs: After reviewing your logs, what kind of commentary would you like to focus on in expanding your reading and thinking skills?

   _____

   _____

   _____

2. AP Reading Comprehension test: What are your strengths? What do you want to work on?

   _____

   _____

   _____

3. Timed Essays: What will you focus on to improve these testing situations?

   _____

   _____

   _____

Portfolio Assignment

*With thanks to Dr. Sheridan Blau, University of California at Santa Barbara

As a record and final product of your effort in this course, you are required to submit a portfolio representing the *quantity* and *quality* of your work in AP English 12. Your portfolio will represent **a collection, a selection, and a reflection**. It will constitute a **collection** of the body of your work, showing the **quantity** of your work for the entire course; it will allow you to identify a selection of the *best work* you have produced—the work that can best show the quality of your reading, writing, and thinking for the course; and it will afford you the opportunity to reflect on what your work has meant to you; what kind of development in your thinking, reading, or speaking it represents; and what you think about what you have accomplished.

Content and Format

The Collection
Your collection may include *everything you write in connection with this course* this semester. This includes your learning log, all your papers in all their drafts, all in-class writing, notes, creative pieces written in class or inspired by the reading, letters or electronic posts you may have written to friends telling about your reading, feedback and personal notes on your own oral presentations, or anything else that can be said to represent the reading, writing, speaking, and thinking you engaged in for AP English 12.

Make sure that your collection is easy to handle (bound between covers or placed securely in a well-marked folder) and organized so that a reader will be able to locate sections and particular materials readily. Label sections clearly and provide a table of contents for the whole collection and possibly for whatever subsections you choose to create. Also provide a rough word count as a measure of the quantity of your writing for the semester.

The Selection
This will represent **your best writing and thinking** for the course and the work that you choose to submit for the most rigorous evaluation. For this section of your portfolio, *select carefully from the work in your collection and feel*

free to revise any writing before you include it in your selection. Remember that two of the goals of this course are flexibility and control. How can you best reveal that you can write in a variety of modes while maintaining control over the conventions of standard English? (Or flout those rules when they serve the purpose of your writing.)

You may select (and revise) whole essays or parts of essays, pieces of in-class writing, or sections of your Daybook. Please word-process any selected Daybook entries you might choose. You may want to photocopy pages of your journal and show them as they were written. Your whole selection may consist of copies of what you regard as your best two or three papers. The only constraint is one of length. **Please limit your selection to 2,500 words or approximately ten pages.**

The Reflection

You are required to include in your portfolio a *general introduction to the whole collection, an introduction to the selection of your best work,* **and** *an introduction to your self-selected sections.*

In the General Introduction:

- ◆ **Choose a quote about writing** that applies to you as a writer. Explain the quote and its application to the body of work represented in the Portfolio.
- ◆ **Describe** the materials and provide any information to aid a reader in an appreciation of the work.
- ◆ **Include a reflection on the meaning of the work as whole** and include its characteristics, qualities, and usefulness to learning.
- ◆ **Estimate** the word count. You should have TWO separate word counts: One for the total writing done for the course and a separate count for the Daybook.

In the Introduction to the Selection:

- ◆ **Describe** the materials and provide any background that may aid the reader in an appreciation of the works.
- ◆ Describe **characteristics, qualities, and the development** from piece to piece.
- ◆ **Reflect on learning gained** in the development of pieces.

In introductions to the other sections:

- **Describe** the section.
- **Reflect** on how the performance in a given area contributed to overall gains (or, possibly hindered gains).

Grading

Your final Portfolio will receive a single grade, which will count as approximately one-third of the final course grade (class participation will count for the rest). A strong portfolio will include a large collection of material, showing evidence of a serious and thoughtful engagement with all or most of the assigned texts, a willingness to take risks with difficult texts, a willingness to read a variety of texts and authors, thoughtful engagement in the assigned writing tasks, participation in a variety of in-class writing exercises, participation in discussions and presentations in class, intellectual honesty throughout, and eight to ten pages of especially thoughtful writing (the selection) that addresses particular texts or problems in reading or criticism. A strong Portfolio will also be well organized and include helpful introductions to and reflections on the work submitted.

Figure A2 Rubric for scoring the End-of-Course Portfolio.

End-of-Course Portfolio Rubric

Name: _____ DUE MAY 19   1/3 course grade: _____

As a general guideline: Use the review of your body of work as a method of both understanding and explaining what you learned with an emphasis on thoughtful engagement.
Place this rubric at the very front of your portfolio.

	Above Standards	Meets Standards	Below Standards
The Collection	Includes all class-related writing including drafts, revisions, seminars, and exercises. Voluminous, complete, has notes to self, others, **shows initiative** to include writings to help explore, understand course materials. Clear evidence of fluency.	Includes all class-related writing, including notes, daily exercises.	Does not reveal engagement with all in-class activities. Scant notes, activities.
	Easy to handle. Bound in such a way as to hold together through transport without effort. Attractive. Shows care and evidence of valuing the work.	Easy to handle. Bound in such a way as to hold together through transport without effort.	Inadequate binding that makes transport difficult, unwieldy.
	Organized around a coherent, logical method. Sections are clearly labeled. A table of contents makes all aspects easy to locate.	There are sections and a table of contents.	Haphazard organization. Sections are not clearly marked or logical. No table of contents.
The Selection _MUST include one analytical paper_	Careful selection showing **evidence of an awareness of excellence** in written communication and clear thinking.	Selections show some merit, though not above the average.	No clear evidence of distinguishing between adequacy and excellence.
	Clean, publishable copies with **revisions** to brought to standards of written language. Rewrites of any Daybook or personal writings if necessary.	Mixture of both clean and illegible entries.	No clean drafts. Illegible.
	Does not exceed ten-page limit. Exhibits _flexibility and control_.	Shows some variety.	Too brief to show range of work.
The Reflection In the _General Introduction_ include a reference to your starting points from your benchmark activities in reading and writing.	_General introduction_ describes materials and supplies any information to aid reader in appreciation of it. Includes reflection of **the meaning of the work as a whole** to individual student, including its _characteristics, qualities, and usefulness_ to learning. INCLUDES SIGNIFICANT RESEARCHED WRITING QUOTE WITH EXPLANATION OF CHOICE. PROVIDES ESTIMATED WORD COUNT. PLUS DAYBOOK WORD COUNT.	General introduction introduces the works and gives scant evidence of the overall meaning of course exercises to improve student composition and analytical skills. No word count. Missing elements circled at left.	Either no introduction or one which only deals with a description of the content of the selections.
	Introduction to Selection describes materials and provides background that may aid the reader in an appreciation of the works. _Describes characteristics, qualities, and development_ from piece to piece. **Reflects on learning gained in development** of pieces. **Shows understanding of problems surmounted** in both composition and analysis. References benchmarks.	Introduction to Selection has only a portion of the expectations for reflection and evidence of growth.	Either no introduction or one which only deals with a description of the content of the selections.
	Introductions to other sections that reflect understanding of performance in any given area and the _usefulness of work to overall gains._	Introductions to other works that do not include a reflection.	No introduction to other sections.

© 2018 Mary Tedrow

Portfolio

To help students improve consistently in their writing and develop an awareness of their reading process, each student will keep a Portfolio in a classroom file that will show progress and areas needing improvement. The most important aspect of the Portfolio, however, is that it engages the student in the process of thinking about writing.

A folder will be provided for you and stored in the classroom for your use. Keep all components of an essay assignment together in the Portfolio. All documents should be full pages. The Portfolio is due each quarter and is worth a class work grade for the quarter.

Documents Needed for Each Essay

◆ A page with the prompt attached.
◆ **All drafts** of the essay (including teacher comments).
◆ Any prewriting or processing notes you made for yourself.
◆ Commentary. When papers are returned, find relevant questions below to answer in regards to the writing assignment.
  – What problems (if any) did I have in understanding the prompt? Explain.
  – What was my "so what" point? Remember, "so what" refers to the main idea the writer is trying to communicate as *you* see it. It is the idea that is universal, timeless, and human. It is what we can learn more about ourselves by understanding. Your thesis statement is NOT your "so what."
  – What could I have done better?
  – Where lapses in organization occurred, what was the cause?
  – Have I introduced my quotations carefully, giving context and weaving them in grammatically and logically?
  – What do I need to take from the teacher's comments for this essay to work on for next time? How do I plan to do that?
  – What did I do better (or worse) this time than last time?
  – If I have chosen to revise this essay, what do I plan to do differently? What significant changes will make the essay much improved over the first draft?
  – What else have I learned about myself as a writer from this essay?

- Do I have a need for teacher conference? Write down what you need to discuss and make an appointment. After the conference, record what was discussed and what you plan to take from the discussion to improve your writing.
- Am I saying what I mean?
- Does this make sense?
- Have I made good connections between ideas?
- Are my ideas logical?

Writing Preface

The purpose of a preface to your writing is to explain the process you have gone through to create your writing. In today's preface please answer the following:

1. What was your original idea for this piece? How did you get it, and did your goal/idea change as you worked on your writing?
2. How did your response group assist you with your personal piece?
3. How did the "exploded moment" change your piece?
4. Which technique did you use to grab the reader's attention with your opening?
5. Assess your final piece. How do you feel about the final product as compared to other writing you have done? What audience do you envision for this writing?

Socratic Seminar

Keep This Explanation Sheet in Your Notebook for Use in the Future

What is Socratic Seminar?

Socratic: of or relating to the Greek philosopher Socrates or his philosophy, especially the method associated with him of seeking the truth by a series of questions and answers. Socrates only taught his students through the introduction of questions.

Seminar: a small class for discussion.

Socratic Seminar: a small class discussion where we search for the truth through answers and questions.

Why Are We Doing This?

Socratic seminar is an attempt to take the focus of the class off of teacher talk and return the hunt for truth and enlightenment to you, the students. It is also an opportunity for everyone to take part in the discussion and share their opinions.

How Does Socratic Seminar Work?

- ◆ Everyone is expected to participate in Socratic Seminar.
- ◆ We will sit in a circle.
- ◆ You will complete a pre-discussion activity before each seminar. Therefore, you will always have something to say. Students who have not completed the assignment will not be permitted to participate.
- ◆ There are two types of participation in the Socratic seminar.

Type I: Effective Participation:	Type II: Ineffective Participation
Citing the text	Interrupting someone
Agreeing or disagreeing with another person	Repeating ideas over and over
Suggesting another interpretation	Dominating the discussion
Asking an appropriate question	Making irrelevant comments
Getting the conversation back on track	Refusing to participate
Questioning a student who has not made a comment in order to include them	Talking to someone while the seminar is going on

How Is Socratic Seminar Graded?

Socratic seminar is graded by the instructor. The teacher keeps track of student responses and comments made. Students will receive negative marks for ineffective participation. An end-of-discussion writing will be turned in that attempts to coalesce the high points of the discussion. This will be returned to the student with the seminar grade.

What Is the Teacher's Role?

The teacher asks the initial questions and keeps track of the people speaking (or not speaking). The teacher will not lead you in conversation or offer answers when nobody else is participating.

Figure A3

Figure A4 Student handout for note taking during the Socratic Seminar.

Name:_____   Date:_____   Period:_____

Note Taking in Socratic Seminar

Directions: Keep track of any comments during the seminar that seem to contain an essential truth or an insight that you had not considered. Identify the speaker.

Today's Topic is_____.

Start time:_____   End Time:_____

COMMENT #1: Participant

COMMENT #4: Participant

COMMENT #2: Participant

COMMENT #5: Participant

COMMENT #3: Participant

Did our talking today make a difference? Explain what primary idea you are taking from seminar today. (Show what you know.)

_____

_____

_____

_____

_____

_____

_____

_____

_____

_____

_____

_____

_____

The Change Paper

In your folder is a record of the scores and goals you set at the beginning of this course. You will use that score sheet, your most recent scores, your reading and writing notebooks, and the initial survey you completed to answer the following questions on your own paper.

Please NUMBER your answers to correspond with the questions below. Answer **all** the questions.

1. How many books did you read during this course? How does that compare to the number of books you read prior to this course?
2. On your own paper, list all of the titles and authors of the books you read. Also list the genres. Use the genre chart in your notebook to make the genre as specific as you can. In the last column, write yes or no to indicate if the book is a college-bound book. Set up a chart like this and record the information under each column heading:

   Title   Author   Genre   College bound (Yes/no)

3. Use a calculator and add up all the pages you have read this year. Include the pages read from the books you abandoned as well as the books you finished. Write the total on your paper. (The answer to this should be a single number.)
4. Compare your scores in Vocabulary, Comprehension, and Grade equivalency from the beginning of the course to the end. **On your own paper, make a chart like the one below:**

	At beginning of course	At end of course
Vocabulary		
Comprehension		
Grade Equivalency		

After Making the Chart, Explain Any Differences You See in Sentences Below the Chart

5. Which is the best book you read this year? Why?
6. Which book did you like the least? Why?
7. How do you decide which books to read? Tell me all the ways. Be specific. What advice could you give to other, less experienced students about selecting books to read?

© 2018 Mary Tedrow

8. Now turn to your Daybook. Count the entries and record the number of writings you completed.
9. Which entry is your longest? (Record the date.) What was the subject of your entry?
10. Read through your entries. Do you see any themes or topics which continually surface? Write about your general impressions of your Daybook as a single book about you.
11. At the beginning of the semester a goal was set reading a minimum of FOUR books by the end of the semester. [If a book is long (over 250 pages) it counts as two books.] ONE of the books HAD TO BE NON-FICTION.

    Look at your list of "Books I Have Read" in your Reader's Notebook.

    Write a paragraph explaining how you handled this goal. Did you meet it? Exceed it? How did you manage to accomplish what you did?

    If your reading score at the beginning was above eleventh grade you were required to read a college-bound book. How did you handle this part of the assignment?
12. You filled out a survey about your reading in the first week of school and it has been returned to you. At the bottom of the survey you set a personal reading goal for this course. You also answered questions about the kinds of reading you do and your attitude toward reading in general. This question has two parts:

    a. How well did you meet your own personal reading goal?
    b. How has your attitude toward reading or the kinds of reading you do changed?

Appendix C

Ancillary Handouts

Rhetorically Accurate VERBS

Here are replacements for the commonly used verb forms of "to be," "to give," "to have," "to say," "to use." Do **NOT** randomly pick a verb. Choose verbs that fit both the meaning and the connotation you wish to employ. Avoid words that feel forced or stuffy. Check dictionary definitions if you are not sure.

Choose From the List of Sentence Patterns Below to *Build Commentary*

Examples

- In "Poem" "word" and "word" + **rhetorically accurate verb** the _____ tone.
- Details such as _____ and _____ direct the speaker's _____ attitude.
- First-person point of view in Alice Walker's "To Hell With Dying" **dictates** the *poignant* tone.
- The **syntactical device of** *repetition* **amplifies** the speaker's *disdainful attitude* toward man's inherent nature.
- Elliot's use of *allusion* **intensifies** the sense of **foreboding** in the passage.

To Use

accepts adopts applies consumes conveys delivers depletes draws upon embraces employs engages entails espouses exercises exerts exhausts expends implements invokes places plies presents produces provides resorts sanctions spends summons undergoes wields

To Say

adjures advances advises asks asserts barks bawls begs bellows beseeches cajoles cheers chimes chortles chuckles commands complains confides counsels cries crows declares decrees demands describes dictates directs discloses divulges elucidates encourages entreats exclaims exhorts explains giggles gripes groans grouses growls grumbles hails hints hisses howls illustrates implies implores inquires insinuates instructs intimates justifies laments laughs leers lisps mandates mews moans mumbles murmurs muses mutters orders pleads ponders pontificates proclaims pronounces proposes queries rationalizes recommends recounts relates reports requests reveals rules screams shouts sighs sings smiles snarls sneers sobs spits states submits suggests thunders titters wails wheezes whimpers whines whispers wonders yaps yelps

To Have

bears boasts commends delivers dictates elicits embraces espouses evinces exhibits expresses holds includes indulges maintains manifests owns posits possesses provokes retains supports tolerates

To Give

addresses administers allots asserts awards bequeaths bestows cedes confers consigns conveys declares delivers discloses dispenses divulges emanates endows grants immolates imparts introduces issues lends posits presents proffers proposes submits transmits vouchsafes yields

To Be

abides acts arises betokens betrays coincides comes about comes to pass compares conjures connotes continues denotes discloses divulges emulates endures exhibits exists exposes follows implies indicates inhabits insinuates intimates lives marks mirrors occurs parallels persists portrays proposes reflects remains represents reveals signals signifies submits subsists suggests symbolizes takes place

Guidelines for Personal Writing

Goals and Objectives

The purpose of this assignment is to give you the opportunity to think in writing about a topic that is of interest to you, an experience that you want to share with others. This assignment is called your personal piece because you determine the topic you want to explore and share with others. Completing this assignment will enable you to experience the writing process from inventing, drafting, revising, editing, to publishing. It is hoped that at least one of the pieces you develop in this course will be extended to an outside audience beyond the confines of this classroom.

The Task

Your task is to write on a topic of concern to you that you want to explore in writing. Consider exploring topics that you are willing to share with others.

The Audience

The initial audience for the personal writing is the other students in the course. An additional audience may be determined by your choice of publication (i.e. a scholarship essay, lyrics for a song to be performed, a poem for a literary magazine, an essay for a magazine or newspaper).

The Process

1. Use your Daybook to explore topics you want to think about in writing. Choose one of them to focus on. Write about it continuously over time. The choice of topic is yours. Others have written about family events or portraits of family members that they want to preserve, events that have had a significant impact on their beliefs and values, experiences that have had an impact on their ways of thinking, significant places that left a lasting impression, or friends and colleagues who have made an impact.
2. Select a format for presenting the topic. This paper may be a short story, historical narrative, personal experience essay, dialogue, letter, poem or lyric, or play. You may want to consider trying different genres that explore the same topic.
3. Share drafts of the personal piece with your reading response group.
4. Revise and edit the piece.
5. Ready the piece for publication.

© 2018 Mary Tedrow

Evaluative Criteria

Be sure your final piece is focused, adequately developed, clearly organized, flows smoothly, uses appropriate word choice, is free of major grammar and mechanical errors, and meets the detailed requirements of the assignment.

Remember that this piece of writing is your opportunity to explore in writing a topic you have been thinking about but never had the time to put in writing. Make this assignment meaningful to you.

Figure A5 Graphic organizer for student pairing to check on progress of research.

Sample Research Check-in with Partner

Student Name: _____

Capstone Project: Midwives

PRIORITY QUESTION	THINGS I KNOW	THINGS I STILL NEED TO FIND OUT
What is midwifery?		
What does a midwife do?		
How do midwives differ from doctors?		

Philosophy Worksheet

You can look at yourself through several lenses. Use the questions below as a way to define your stance toward your world. This is a worksheet in the truest sense: you are to work your way through the different aspects of your life. *Think* in writing about how you feel about each of these areas of your life. (More thought = more writing. Think extensively.) You will need these definitions in order to compare the "world" of each piece of literature to your own.

1. What is your view of a deity? (If the universe is a watch, what/ who is the watchmaker?)

    _____

    _____

2. What is your view of society? (Think in terms of the organization of humanity.)

    _____

    _____

3. What is your view of nature? (Consider how you characterize the natural world.)

    _____

    _____

4. What is your view of man? (Gods? Demi-gods? Pitiful failures?)

    _____

    _____

5. What is your place in history? (What shifts or changes are occurring in the world? What do think you might bear witness to before death?)

    _____

    _____

6. **Find a quote** that reflects your view of the world. You may use Internet resources. Copy the quote below and attribute it to the speaker.

    _____

    _____

Philosophy in *BRIEF*

There are many "schools of thought." Here are a few to consider as you think about your own view of the world. Definitions are from www.geniscarreras.com as part of Genís Carreras's *Philographics* minimalist art project. (Carreras is an artist who specializes in simple shapes. His poster art attaches a shape to each of the philosophies below.)

Absolutism: the position that within a particular school of thought, all different perspectives are either absolutely true or absolutely false.

Atheism: the absence of belief that gods or deities exist.

Authoritarianism: the organization of society through strong, often oppressive measures against its people.

Determinism: the proposition that all events, including those of human thoughts, are causally determined by an unbroken chain of prior events.

Dogma: the inflexible adherence to a rigid doctrine or ideology, not open to rational argument or debate.

Dualism: the conviction that all concepts within the world fundamentally consist of two contrasting qualities such as good and evil or body and mind.

Empiricism: the scientific doctrine stating that all knowledge ultimately comes from sensory experience and observable evidence rather than intuition or preconceived ideas.

Existentialism: the idea that all philosophical thought must begin with the experiences of the individual, and it is up to the individual to give meaning and authenticity to their own experience.

Free Will: the ability of conscious agents to be free to make their own decisions, free of any social, moral, or political constraints.

Hedonism: the ethical position that pleasure is the ultimate goal and greatest good, and should be the central aim of all decisions made.

Holism: the theory that the properties of a system cannot be understood by the sum of its parts alone, but by how the system behaves as a whole.

Humanism: a range of ethical views that consider human nature to be the source of morality.

Idealism: the philosophical view that asserts that reality is fundamentally based on, and shaped by, ideas and mental experiences, rather than material forces.

Nihilism: the philosophical view that the world, and human existence in particular, is without meaning, purpose, or value.

Marxism: a set of philosophical, political, and economic positions based on the work of Karl Marx, centered upon a materialist interpretation of history and critique of capitalism.

Positivism: the position that the only authentic knowledge is that acquired through scientific means.

Rationalism: the theory that human reason can be the source of all knowledge.

Realism: the belief that reality exists independently of our own observation or perception.

Reductionism: the idea that the nature of complex things can always be reduced and explained by simpler, more fundamental truths.

Relativism: the assertion that no belief can be said to have absolute truth, having value only within a certain context for frame of reference.

Skepticism: the method of practicing doubt when regarding what is held as knowledge.

Solipsism: the view that only direct mental experience is certain, as things external to one's own mind cannot be known.

Theism: the belief that a god or deity is present and active in the universe.

Utilitarianism: the school of ethics that strives towards the maximization of welfare for the maximum number of people.

The Personal Statement of *Your Name*

This is what your personal statement should look like. Use the heading above only. Write the paper in 10- or 12-point fonts. Choose a standard font like Times New Roman, Arial, or Garamond. According to our business teachers, you may write in first or third person (as if you are writing about someone else). Do the following:

- ◆ Double space the body of the paper.
- ◆ Write about yourself. Consider the following things:
  - − What do you value? (Look at the list from the Dream Job.)
  - − What skills and strengths do you have? (from the Great Experience)
  - − What are you bringing to a school or workplace that is unique to you?
  - − Why do you event WANT the job or to go to college? What do you hope to gain from it?

In everything you write, be as SPECIFIC as possible. In other words, mention events, activities, and experiences that demonstrate your qualities.

The personal statement should be one page in length. This is the standard expectation. Parts of your personal statement may come in handy for cover letters for job applications or statements about yourself when applying for scholarships, social groups, mentorship programs, or internships.

Write the personal statement once and then modify it to suit later purposes. Here's another tip for those who like to think ahead: keep your Personal Statement on your computer and update it from time to time to suit your changing awareness of yourself and your interests and abilities. If you are prepared, then you will be ready at a moment's notice to take advantage of any great opportunities which come your way.

Figure A6 Strengths and Skills vocabulary for student use during the Great Experience writing.

Strengths & Skills Checklist

ANALYZE	EVALUATOR	RESEARCH	YOUR SKILLS
Abstracting	Auditing	Inspecting	
Conceptualizing	Estimating	Investigating	
Analyzing	Evaluating	Observing	
Appraising	Examining	Reading	
Classifying	Interviewing	Researching	
Dealing With Unknowns	Monitoring	Reviewing	
Interpreting	Questioning	Updating	
COMMUNICATE - human relations-motivate-negotiate	**COMMUNICATE -** inform-instruct-teach-train	**COMMUNICATE -** perform-persuade	
Advising	Copywriting	Acting	
Coaching	Editing	Dramatizing	
Confronting	Explaining	Entertaining	
Counseling	Proposals	Fundraising	
Group Facilitating	Rewriting	Lobbying	
Expressing Feelings	Speaking	Politicking	
Tolerating	Supervising	Promoting	
Listening	Training	Recruiting	
Motivating	Translating	Representing	
Negotiating	Writing	Selling	
COORDINATE	**ORGANIZE**	**PLAN**	
Assembling	Arranging	Processing	
Compiling	Delegating	Timing	
Coordinating	Organizing	Planning	
CREATE	**DEVELOP**	**FORESIGHT**	
Creating	Developing	Anticipating	
Designing	Making Layouts	Imagining	
Displaying	Preparing		
Drawing/Sketching	Refining		
CONTROL	**PRECISE**	**TECHNICAL**	
Controlling	Experimenting	Memorizing	
Budgeting	Handling Details	Programming	
Calculating	Mathematical Modeling	Recording	
DECIDE	**MANAGER**	**LEAD**	
Administering	Disciplining	Envisioning	
Deciding	Managing	Directing	
Delegating	Supervising	Initiating	
EXECUTE	**OPERATE**	**SERVING**	
Constructing	Moving With Dexterity	Protecting	
Distributing	Operating	Rehabilitating	
Repairing	Working Outdoors	Serving	
PERSERVERE	**RISK/CHALLENGE**	**PROBLEM SOLVE**	
Enduring	Dealing With Pressure	Handling Complaints	
Perservering	Confronting	Mediating	
Protecting	Repeating	Troubleshooting	
	Risking		

© 2018 Mary Tedrow

The College Essay

Below Are the College Essay Questions for Applicants in the 2016–2017 School Year

All below come from the Common Application (used by many colleges and universities, including William and Mary and Mary Washington College). The instructions say, "Write an essay (250–650 words) on one of the options listed below."

1. *Some students have a background, identity, interest, or talent that is so meaningful they believe their application would be incomplete without it.* If this sounds like you, then please share your story.
2. *The lessons we take from failure can be fundamental to later success.* Recount an incident or time when you experienced failure. How did it affect you, and what did you learn from the experience?
3. Reflect on a time when you challenged a belief or idea. What prompted you to act? Would you make the same decision again?
4. *Describe a problem you've solved or a problem you'd like to solve. It can be an intellectual challenge, a research query, an ethical dilemma—anything that is of personal importance, no matter the scale. Explain its significance to you and what steps you took or could be taken to identify a solution.*
5. Discuss an accomplishment or event, formal or informal, that marked your transition from childhood to adulthood within your culture, community, or family.

U.Va. also asks for a second essay on a topic of your choice. Directions and prompts are below:

Required Essays for First-Year Applicants Only:

1. Answer the question that corresponds to the school you selected above. Limit your answer to a half page or roughly 250 words.
   College of Arts and Sciences: What work of art, music, science, mathematics, or literature has surprised, unsettled, or challenged you, and in what way?
   School of Engineering and Applied Sciences: If you were given funding for a small engineering project that would make everyday life better for one friend or family member, what would you do?

School of Architecture: Describe an instance or place where you have been inspired by architecture or design.

School of Nursing: Discuss experiences that led you to choose the School of Nursing.

Kinesiology Program: Discuss experiences that led you to choose the kinesiology major.

2. Answer one of the following questions in a half page or roughly 250 words:

   – What's your favorite word and why?

   – We are a community with quirks, both in language and in traditions. Describe one of your quirks and why it is part of who you are.

   – Student self-governance, which encourages student investment and initiative, is a hallmark of the UVA culture. In her fourth year at UVA, Laura Nelson was inspired to create Flash Seminars, one-time classes which facilitate high-energy discussion about thought-provoking topics outside of traditional coursework. If you created a Flash Seminar, what idea would you explore and why?

   – UVA students paint messages on Beta Bridge when they want to share information with our community. What would you paint on Beta Bridge, and why is this your message?

In the Prompts Below the Name of the School Indicates Where the Essay Question Came From

Assume that essays should range from 250–500 words when not otherwise indicated.

- How will you explore your intellectual and academic interests at the University of Pennsylvania? Please answer this question give the specific undergraduate school to which you are applying (400–650 words). (University of Pennsylvania)
- Other parts of your application give us a sense for how you might contribute to Northwestern. But we also want to consider how Northwestern will contribute to your interests and goals. In 300 words or less, help us understand what aspects of Northwestern appeal most to you, and how you'll make use of specific resources and opportunities here. (Northwestern University)
- The Bryn Mawr Honor Code and Self-Government Association (SGA) affirm the importance of our academic and social

communities. In your response please reflect on how you see the Honor Code and/or SGA shaping your experience at Bryn Mawr. (Bryn Mawr College)

♦ Optional Question 2: Please elaborate on how you have familiarized yourself with Washington and Lee University and what led to your decision to apply (250 words maximum). (Washington and Lee University)

♦ Duke University seeks a talented, engaged study body that embodies the wide range of human experience; we believe that the diversity of our students makes our community stronger. If you'd like to share a perspective you bring or experiences you've had to help us understand you better—perhaps related to a community you belong to, your sexual orientation or gender identity, or your family or cultural background—we encourage you to do so. Real people are reading your application, and we want to do our best to understand and appreciate the real people applying to Duke (250 words maximum). (Duke University)

♦ Candidates respond to all three essay topics. There is a 100-word minimum and a 250-word maximum for each essay. 1. Stanford students possess an intellectual vitality. Reflect on an idea or experience that has been important to your intellectual development. 2. Virtually all of Stanford's undergraduates live on campus. Write a note to your future roommate that reveals something about you or that will help your roommate—and us—know you better. 3. What matters to you, and why? (Stanford University)